P9-DFX-075

simply baby

Debbie Bliss   photography by Tim Evan-Cook

simply baby

20 adorable knits for baby's first two years

Trafalgar Square Publishing
North Pomfret, Vermont

ALEXANDRIA LIBRARY
ALEXANDRIA, VA 22304

First published in the United States of America in 2006
by **Trafalgar Square Publishing**
North Pomfret, Vermont 05053.

Printed in Singapore

Originally published in the United Kingdom in 2006 by
Quadrille Publishing Limited, London.

Text and project designs
© 2006 Debbie Bliss
Photography, design, and layout
© 2006 Quadrille Publishing Limited

All rights reserved.

The designs in this book are copyright and must not
be made for resale.

Library of Congress Control Number: 2006902664

ISBN-13: 978-1-57076-334-2
ISBN-10: 1-57076-334-8

Editorial Director **Jane O'Shea**
Creative Director **Mary Evans**
Project Editor **Lisa Pendreigh**
Editorial Assistant **Andrew Bayliss**
Photographer **Tim Evan-Cook**
Stylist **Julie Mansfield**
Production Director **Vincent Smith**
Production Controller **Ruth Deary**

10 9 8 7 6 5 4 3 2 1

First edition

contents

introduction

Although in my career I design for both adults and children, I have to admit that there is something very special about creating hand knits for babies. I love every part of the process of putting together a collection, from the very initial stages when I first begin to think about the styles, shapes, and sizes to the culmination of it all when I see the collection come together and photographed on the children.

In **Simply Baby** I have created a range of easy knit styles that also introduce the less experienced knitter to texture and colorwork with simple cables, Fair Isle, and intarsia. One of the joys of knitting small garments is that you can quickly see your project grow and take shape and feel less overwhelmed at tackling new techniques. A small Fair Isle border on a cardigan or an easy cable and rib tank top seems manageable and not too challenging when you are beginning to develop your skills in new areas.

Designing for children is very different from designing for men and women. Although style is still very important, wearability and comfort also have to play an essential part. I tend to create jackets and cardigans rather than sweaters for tiny babies because as they cannot sit up at that stage it can be difficult to put garments on without causing discomfort. Sweaters should have envelope necks or shoulder buttons so that they can be easily pulled over a baby's head.

Fiber content is paramount when choosing a yarn. Not only should it be soft against the skin but safe to wear. Yarns such as angora, alpaca, and mohair have long, detachable fibers and are not suitable for baby wear.

I always include not only the age size in the pattern but also the knitted measurements of the design. Based on your knowledge of the child you are knitting for, you may want to choose to make a smaller or larger size. If you feel some of my measurements seem larger than you would expect, measure the size of a garment they are already wearing and you may be surprised at the result as it is important to allow for body ease.

Finally, there are wonderful, sophisticated palettes of color that are available to choose from for your knits, gone are the days when choice was limited to sickly pastels or baby brights. As you can see, I have chosen duck egg blues, chocolate browns, and dusky pinks and lilacs, enlivened by lime and apple green. But if you would prefer to make a more personal choice, don't forget soft grays, smart navy, and terra-cottas.

yarns

types of yarns

When choosing a yarn for babies or children, it is essential that you work with a fiber that is soft and gentle against a baby's skin. Babies are not able to tell you if a collar is rough against their neck or if cuffs are irritating their wrists, and since older children are often more used to the lightweight freedom of fleeces, they can be resistant to hand knits that they may consider scratchy and uncomfortable.

The yarns I have chosen for the patterns in this book are cashmere combined with either cotton or merino wool, giving softness and durability, and a pure cotton. Although they create fabrics that are sumptously soft to wear, most importantly all these yarns are machine washable.

When knitting a garment, whenever possible try to buy the yarn stated in the pattern. All these designs have been created with a specific yarn in mind: the Hooded Jacket is worked in a softer yarn to gently frame a baby's face, while the Roll Edge Jacket is made in a natural cotton to give it the necessary sturdiness to maintain its shape—a floppier fiber or a synthetic yarn would create a limp fabric. From an esthetic point of view, the clarity of a subtle stitch pattern may be lost if a garment is knitted in an inferior yarn.

However, there may be occasions when a knitter needs to substitute a yarn—if there is an allergy to wool, for example—and so the following is a guideline to making the most informed choices.

Always buy a yarn that is the same weight as that given in the pattern: replace a double knitting with a double knitting, for example, and check that the gauge of both yarns is the same.

Where you are substituting a different fiber, be aware of the design. A cable pattern knitted in cotton when worked in wool will pull in because of the greater elasticity of the yarn and so the fabric will become narrower; this will alter the proportions of the garment.

Check the yardage of the yarn. Yarns that weigh the same may have different lengths in the ball or hank, so you may need to buy more or less yarn.

Here are descriptions of my yarns and a guide to their weights and types:

Debbie Bliss baby cashmerino:
A lightweight yarn between a fingering and a double-knitting yarn.
55% merino wool, 33% microfiber, 12% cashmere.
Approximately 137yd (1³/₄oz/50g) per ball.
Debbie Bliss cashmerino aran:
55% merino wool, 33% microfiber, 12% cashmere.
Approximately 98yd (1³/₄oz/50g) per ball.
Debbie Bliss cashmerino double knitting:
55% merino wool, 33% microfiber, 12% cashmere.
Approximately 120yd (1³/₄oz/50g) per ball.

Debbie Bliss cotton cashmere:
85% cotton,15% cashmere.
Approximately 104yd (1³/₄oz/50g) per ball.
Debbie Bliss cotton double knitting:
100% cotton.
Approximately 92yd (1³/₄oz/50g) per ball.

buying yarn

The yarn label will carry all the essential information you need as to gauge, needle size, weight, and yardage. Importantly it will also have the dye lot. Yarns are dyed in batches or lots, which can vary considerably. As your retailer may not have the same dye lot later on, buy all your yarn for a project at the same time. If you know that sometimes you use more yarn than that quoted in the pattern, buy extra. If it is not possible to buy all the yarn you need with the same dye lot, use the different ones where it will not show as much—on a neck or border for example—as a change of dye lot across a main piece is more likely to show.

It is also a good idea at the time of buying the yarn to check the pattern and make sure that you already have the needles you will require. If not, buy them now because it will save a lot of frustration when you get home.

garment care

Taking care of your hand knits is important because you want them to look good for as long as possible. Correct washing is particularly important for baby garments as they need to be washed often.

Check the yarn label for washing instructions to see whether the yarn is hand or machine washable, and if it is the latter, at what temperature it should be washed.

Most hand knits should be dried flat on an absorbent cloth, such as a towel, to soak up any moisture. Laying them flat in this way gives you an opportunity to pat the garment back into shape if it has become pulled around in the washing machine. Even if you are in a hurry, do not be tempted to dry your knits near a direct heat source, such as a radiator.

As baby garments are small, you may prefer to hand wash them. Use a washing agent that is specifically designed for knitwear since this will be kinder to the fabric. Use warm rather than hot water and handle the garment gently without rubbing or wringing. Let the water out of the sink and then gently squeeze out the excess water. Do not lift out a water-logged knit as the weight of the water will pull it out of shape. You may need to remove more moisture by rolling it in a towel. Dry flat as before.

knitting
basics

cast on

slip knot

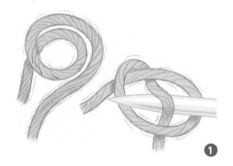 

Your first step when beginning to knit is to work a foundation row called a cast-on. Without this row you cannot begin to knit.

There are several methods of casting on, each can be suited to a particular purpose or is chosen because the knitter feels comfortable with that particular technique. The two examples shown here are the ones I have found to be the most popular, the thumb and the cable methods.

In order to work a cast-on edge, you must first make a slip knot.

1 Wind the yarn around the fingers on your left hand to make a circle of yarn as shown above. With the knitting needle, pull a loop of the yarn attached to the ball through the yarn circle on your fingers.

2 Pull both ends of the yarn to tighten the slip knot on the knitting needle. You are now ready to begin, using either of the following cast-on techniques.

thumb cast-on

The thumb cast-on is a one needle method that produces a flexible edge, which makes it particularly useful when using nonelastic yarns such as cotton. The "give" in it also makes it a good one to use where the edge will turn back, as on Roll Edge Jacket (see page 132).

Unlike two-needle methods you are working toward the yarn end, which means you have to predict the length you need to cast on the required amount of stitches. Otherwise you may find you do not have enough yarn to complete the last few stitches and have to start all over again. If you are unsure, always allow for more yarn than you think you need because you can use what is left over for sewing seams.

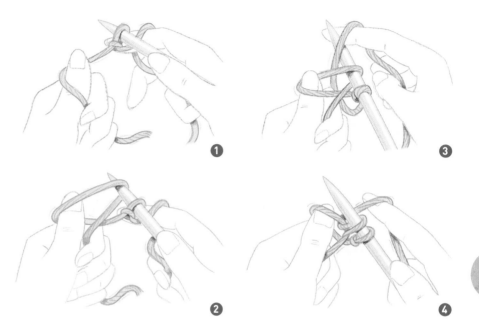

1 Make a slip knot as shown opposite, leaving a long tail. With the slip knot on the needle in your right hand and the yarn that comes from the ball over your index finger, wrap the tail end of the yarn over your left thumb from front to back, holding the yarn in your palm with your fingers.

2 Insert the knitting needle upward through the yarn loop on your left thumb.

3 With the right index finger, wrap the yarn from the ball up and over the point of the knitting needle.

4 Draw the yarn through the loop on your thumb to form a new stitch on the knitting needle. Then, let the yarn loop slip off your left thumb and pull the loose end to tighten up the stitch. Repeat these steps until the required number of stitches have been cast on.

cast on

cable cast-on

The cable cast-on method uses two needles and is particularly good for ribbed edges, as it provides a sturdy, but still elastic, edge. Since you need to insert the needle between the stitches and pull the yarn through to create another stitch, make sure that you do not make the new stitch too tight. The cable method is one of the most widely used cast-ons.

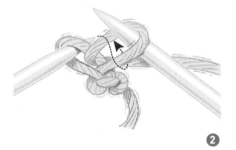

1 Make a slip knot as shown on the previous page. Hold the knitting needle with the slip knot in your left hand and insert the right-hand needle from left to right and from front to back through the slip knot. Wrap the yarn from the ball up and over the point of the right-hand needle as shown.

2 With the right-hand needle, draw a loop through the slip knot to make a new stitch. Do not drop the stitch from the left-hand needle, but instead slip the new stitch onto the left-hand needle as shown.

3 Next, insert the right-hand needle between the two stitches on the left-hand needle and wrap the yarn around the point of the right-hand needle.

4 Pull the yarn through to make a new stitch, and then place the new stitch on the left-hand needle, as before. Repeat the last two steps until the required number of stitches have been cast on.

knit

The knit and purl stitches form the basis of almost all knitted fabrics. The knit stitch is the easiest to learn and is the first stitch you will create. When worked continuously, it forms a reversible fabric called garter stitch. You can recognize garter stitch by the horizontal ridges formed at the top of the knitted loops.

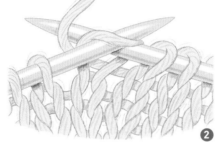

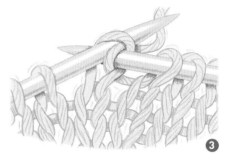

1 With the cast-on stitches on the needle in your left hand, insert the right-hand needle from left to right and from front to back through the first cast-on stitch.

2 Take the yarn from the ball on your index finger (the working yarn) around the point of the right-hand needle.

3 Draw the right-hand needle and yarn through the stitch, thus forming a new stitch on the right-hand needle, and at the same time slip the original stitch off the left-hand needle. Repeat these steps until all the stitches from the left-hand needle have been worked. One knit row has now been completed.

&purl

After the knit stitch, you will move on to the purl stitch. If you work the purl stitch continuously it forms the same fabric as garter stitch. However, if you alternate the purl rows with knit rows, it creates stockinette stitch, which is the most widely used knitted fabric.

1 With the yarn at the front of the work, insert the right-hand needle from the right to the left into the front of the first stitch on the left-hand needle.

2 Then take the yarn from the ball on your index finger (the working yarn) around the point of the right-hand needle.

3 Draw the right-hand needle and the yarn through the stitch, thus forming a new stitch on the right-hand needle, and at the same time slip the original stitch off the left-hand needle. Repeat these steps until all the stitches have been worked. One purl row has now been completed.

increase

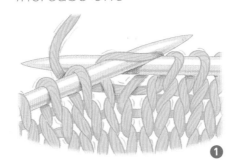

Increases are used to add to the width of the knitted fabric by creating more stitches. They are worked, for example, when shaping sleeves up the length of the arm or when additional stitches are needed after a ribbed edging. Some increases are invisible, while others are worked away from the edge of the work and are meant to be seen in order to give decorative detail. Most knitting patterns will tell you which type of increase to make.

1 Insert the right-hand needle into the front of the next stitch, then knit the stitch but leave it on the left-hand needle.

2 Insert the right-hand needle into the back of the same stitch and knit it. Then slip the original stitch off the needle. Now you have made an extra stitch on the right-hand needle.

1 Insert the left-hand needle from front to back under the horizontal strand between the stitch just worked on the right-hand needle and the first stitch on the left-hand needle.

2 Knit into the back of the loop to twist it, and to prevent a hole. Drop the strand from the left-hand needle. This forms a new stitch on the right-hand needle.

yarn over

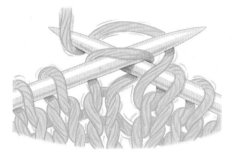

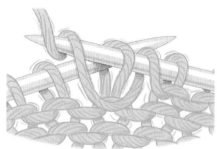

yarn over between knit stitches
Bring the yarn forward between the two needles, from the back to the front of the work. Taking the yarn over the needle to do so, knit the next stitch.

yarn over between purl stitches
Bring the yarn over the needle to the back, then between the two needles to the front. Then purl the next stitch.

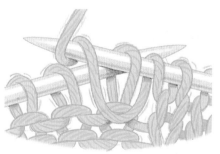

yarn over between a purl and a knit
Take the yarn from the front over the needle to the back. Then knit the next stitch.

yarn over between a knit and a purl
Bring the yarn forward between the two needles from the back to the front of the work, and take it over the top of the needle to the back again and then forward between the needles. Then purl the next stitch.

bindoff

Binding off is used to finish off your knitted piece so that the stitches don't unravel. It is also used to decrease more than one stitch at a time, such as when shaping armholes, neckbands, and buttonholes. It is important that a bind-off is firm but elastic, particularly when binding off around a neckband, to ensure that it can be pulled easily over the head. Unless told otherwise, bind off in the pattern used in the piece.

knit bind-off

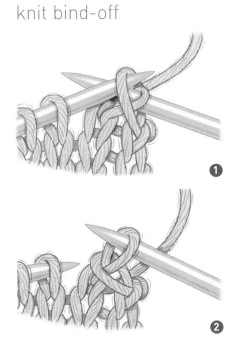

1 Knit two stitches. Insert the left-hand needle into the first stitch knitted on the right-hand needle and lift this stitch over the second stitch and off the right-hand needle.

2 One stitch is now on the right-hand needle. Knit the next stitch. Repeat the first step until all the stitches have been bound off. Pull the yarn through the last stitch to fasten off.

purl bind-off

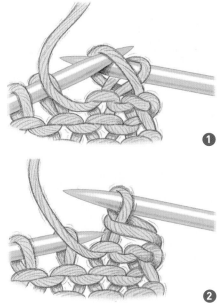

1 Purl two stitches. Insert the left-hand needle into the back of the first stitch worked on the right-hand needle and lift this stitch over the second stitch and off the right-hand needle.

2 One stitch is now on the right-hand needle. Purl the next stitch. Repeat the first step until all the stitches have been bound off. Pull the yarn through the last stitch to fasten off.

decrease

knit 2 together   purl 2 together   slip stitch over

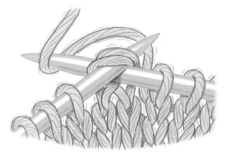

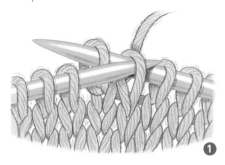

Knit 2 together ("k2tog" or "dec one")
On a knit row, insert the right-hand needle from left to right through the next two stitches on the left-hand needle and knit them together. One stitch has been decreased.

Purl 2 together ("p2tog" or "dec one")
On a purl row, insert the right-hand needle from right to left through the next two stitches on the left-hand needle. Then purl them together. One stitch has been decreased.

Decreases are used to make the fabric narrower by getting rid of stitches on the needle. They are worked to make an opening for a neckline or shape a sleeve cap. As with increases, they can be used to create decorative detail, often around a neck edge. Increases and decreases are used together to create lace patterns.

Slip 1, knit 1, pass slipped stitch over ("skp")
1 Insert the right-hand needle into the next stitch on the left-hand needle and slip it onto the right-hand needle without knitting it. Knit the next stitch. Then insert the left-hand needle into the slipped stitch as shown.

2 With the left-hand needle, lift the slipped stitch over the knitted stitch as shown and off the right-hand needle.

reading patterns

To those unfamiliar with knitting patterns, they can appear to be written in a strange, alien language! However, as you become used to the terminology, you will see that they have a logic and consistency that you will soon become familiar with.

Do not be too concerned if you read through a pattern first and are confused by parts of it, as some instructions make more sense when your stitches are on the needle and you are at that stage in the piece. However, it is sometimes a good idea to check with your yarn store whether your skill level is up to a particular design. This can prevent frustration later on.

Figures for larger sizes are given in parentheses (). Where only one figure appears, it means that those numbers apply to all sizes. Figures in brackets [] are to be worked the number of times stated after the brackets. Where 0 appears, no stitches or rows are worked for this size.

When you follow the pattern, it is important that you consistently use the right stitches or rows for your size. Switching between sizes can be avoided if you mark your size throughout with a highlighting pen on a photocopy of the pattern.

Before starting your project, check the size and the knitted measurements that are quoted for that size. You may want to make a smaller or larger garment depending on the proportions of the wearer it is intended for.

The quantities of yarn quoted in the instructions are based on the yarn used by the knitter of the original garment, and therefore all amounts should be considered approximate. For example, if that knitter has used almost all of the last ball, it may be that another knitter with a slightly different gauge has to start another ball to complete the garment. A slight variation in gauge can therefore make the difference between using fewer or more balls than that stated in the pattern.

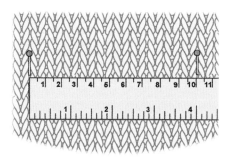

gauge

Every knitting pattern gives a gauge—the number of stitches and rows to a 4-inch square that should be obtained with the quoted yarn, needle size, and stitch pattern. It is important to check your gauge before starting your project. A slight variation can alter the proportions of the finished garment and the look of the fabric. A gauge that is too loose will produce an uneven and unstable fabric that can drop or lose its shape after washing, while a gauge that is too tight can make a hard, inelastic fabric.

Making a gauge square

Use the same needles, yarn, and stitch pattern quoted in the gauge note in the pattern. Knit a sample at least 5 inches square to get the most accurate result. Smooth out the finished sample on a flat surface, making sure you are not stretching it out. To check the stitch gauge, place a tape measure or ruler horizontally on the sample and mark 4 inches with pins. Count the number of stitches between the pins. To check the row gauge, mark 4 inches with pins vertically as before and count the number of rows. If the number of stitches and rows is greater than that quoted in the pattern, your gauge is tighter and you should try changing to a larger needle size and make another gauge square. If there are fewer stitches and rows, your gauge is looser and you should try again on a smaller needle size. The stitch gauge is the most important to get right, as the number of stitches in a pattern are set, but the length is often given as a measurement rather than in rows and you may be able to work more or fewer rows.

abbreviations

The general abbreviations used in this book are listed on this page. Any special abbreviations needed are provided at the beginning of the individual patterns.

Standard abbreviations

alt = alternate

beg = begin(ning)

cont = continu(e)(ing)

dec = decreas(e)(ing)

foll = follow(s)(ing)

inc = increas(e)(ing)

k = knit

M1 = make one stitch by picking up the loop lying between the stitch just worked and the next stitch and working into the back of it

patt = pattern; or work in pattern

p = purl

psso = pass slipped stitch over

rem = remain(s)(ing)

rep = repeat(s)(ing)

skp = slip 1, knit 1, pass slipped stitch over

sl = slip

st(s) = stitch(es)

St st = stockinette stitch

tbl = through back of loop(s)

tog = together

yo = yarn over right needle to make a new stitch

27

stitch types

Once you have mastered the knit and purl stitches, you can combine the two to create an endless variety of stitch patterns. Each stitch pattern has its own character, and most knitters have a particular favorite. Mine is seed stitch, which I use in many of my designs.

garter stitch

Garter stitch is made of all knit rows, which create a dense, reversible fabric. It is particularly good for plain garments without borders as the fabric lies flat and doesn't curl up at the edges. Garter stitch gives new knitters the opportunity to create simple garments without ribbing or borders.

Cast on any number of stitches.
Knit every row.
Repeat this row to form garter stitch.

stockinette stitch

Stockinette stitch, the most commonly used pattern, is worked using alternate knit and purl rows. The purl row is considered to be the wrong side, but you can make either side the right or wrong side depending on the effect you want. When the purl side of stockinette stitch is used as the right side, the fabric is called reverse stockinette stitch.

Cast on any number of stitches.
1st row (right side) Knit.
2nd row (wrong side) Purl.

Repeat the first and second rows to form stockinette stitch.

single rib or 1 x 1 rib

Ribbing is made by alternating vertical columns of knit and purl stitches. The knitter changes from knit to purl within the row. Ribbing can be used as an allover pattern, but it's elasticity makes it perfect for borders such as neckbands and cuffs because it stretches and springs back into shape to fit the body.

Cast on an even number of stitches.
1st row *K1, p1, repeat from * to end.
Repeat this row to form single rib.

double rib or 2 x 2 rib

Cast on a multiple of 4 stitches, plus 2.
1st row K2,*p2, k2, repeat from * to end.
2nd row P2,*k2, p2, repeat from * to end.
Repeat the first and second rows to form double rib.

seed stitch

Seed stitch is one of the most attractive of the simple stitch patterns. The reversible fabric is achieved by working knit and purl stitches that alternate vertically and horizontally. It works well as a stand-alone pattern but is also a good alternative to ribbing to provide decorative detail.

Cast on an uneven number of stitches.
1st row K1,*p1, k1, repeat from * to end.
Repeat this row to form seed stitch.

seed stitch

stockinette stitch

garter stitch

double rib

single rib

cables

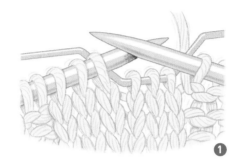

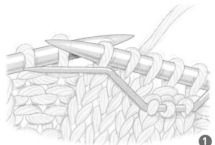

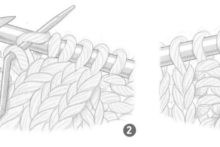

31

Cables are formed by the simple technique of crossing one set of stitches over another. Stitches are held on a cable needle (a short double-pointed needle) at the back or front of the work while the same amount of stitches is worked from the left-hand needle. Simple cables form a vertical twisted rope of stockinette stitch on a background of reverse stockinette stitch and tend to be worked over four or six stitches.

1 Slip the first three cable stitches purlwise off the left-hand needle and onto the cable needle. Leave the cable needle at the back of the work, then knit the next three stitches on the left-hand needle, keeping the yarn tight to prevent a gap from forming in the knitting.

2 Knit the three stitches directly from the cable needle, or if preferred, slip the three stitches from the cable needle back onto the left-hand needle and then knit them. This completes the cable cross.

1 Slip the first three cable stitches purlwise off the left-hand needle and onto the cable needle. Leave the cable needle at the front of the work, then knit the next three stitches on the left-hand needle, keeping the yarn tight to prevent a gap from forming in the knitting.

2 Knit the three stitches directly from the cable needle, or if preferred, slip the three stitches from the cable needle back onto the left-hand needle and then knit them. This completes the cable cross.

intarsia

vertical

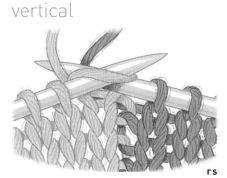

rs

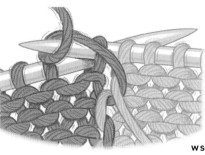

ws

right diagonal

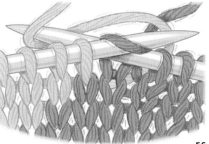

rs

ws

Intarsia is used when you are working with larger areas of usually isolated color, such as when knitting motifs. If the yarn not in use was stranded or woven behind, it could show through to the front or pull in the colorwork. In intarsia you use separate strands or small balls of yarn for each color area and then twist them together where they meet to prevent a gap forming.

Changing colors on a vertical line
If the two color areas are forming a vertical line, to change colors on a knit row drop the color you were using. Pick up the new color and wrap it around the dropped color as shown, then continue with the new color. Twist the yarns together on knit and purl rows in this same way at vertical-line color changes.

Changing colors on a right diagonal
If the two color areas are forming a right diagonal line, on a knit row drop the color you were using. Pick up the new color and wrap it around the dropped color as shown, then continue with the new color. Twist the yarns together on knit rows only at right-diagonal color changes.

left diagonal

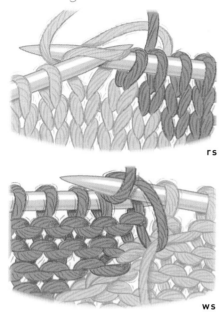

rs

ws

working from a chart

■ M teal   ■ A pale blue   ■ B indigo   ■ C lime   ■ D burgundy   ■ E ecru

21
19
17
15
13
11
9
7
5
3
1

└── **12 st patt repeat** ──┘

33

Changing colors on a left diagonal
If the two color areas are forming
a left diagonal line, on a purl row drop
the color you were using. Pick up
the new color and wrap it around
the color just dropped as shown,
then continue with the new color. Twist
the yarns together on purl rows only at
left-diagonal color changes.

Most color patterns are worked from a
chart rather than set out in the text.
Each square represents a stitch and
row and the symbol or color within it
will tell you which color to use. There
will be a key listing the symbols used
and the colors they represent.

   Unless stated otherwise, the first
row of the chart is worked from right
to left and represents the first right
side row of your knitting. The second
chart row represents the second
and wrong side row and is read and
worked from left to right.

   If the color pattern is a repeated
design, as in Fair Isle, the chart will
tell you how many stitches are in each
repeat. You will repeat these stitches

as many times as is required. At each
side of the repeat there may be edge
stitches, these are only worked at the
beginning and end of the rows and
they indicate where you need to start
and end for the piece you are knitting.
Most color patterns are worked in
stockinette stitch.

stranding

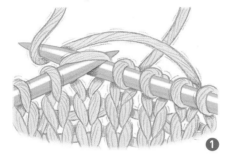

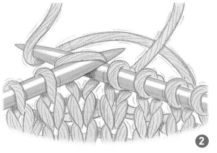

Stranding is used when color is worked over a small amount of stitches where using two colors in a row. The color you are not using is left hanging on the wrong side of the work and then picked up when it is needed again. This creates strands at the back of the work called floats. Care must be taken so that they are not pulled too tightly as this will pucker the fabric. By picking up the yarn over and under one another you will prevent it from tangling.

1 On a right-side (knit) row, to change colors drop the color you were using. Pick up the new color, take it over the top of the dropped color, and start knitting with it.

2 To change back to the old color, drop the color you were knitting with. Pick up the old color, take it under the dropped color, and knit to the next color change, and so on.

1 On a wrong-side (purl) row, to change colors drop the color you were using. Pick up the new color, take it over the top of the dropped color, and start purling with it.

2 To change back to the old color, drop the color you were knitting with. Pick up the old color, take it under the dropped color, and purl to the next color change, and so on.

&weaving in

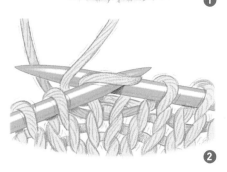

35

When there are more than four stitches between a color change, the floats are too long and this makes the fabric inflexible. The long strands can also catch when wearing the garment, particularly on the inside of a sleeve. By weaving in, the yarn not in use is caught up before the next color change, thus shortening the float. Sometimes, depending on the color pattern, a combination of both stranding and weaving can be used.

1 To weave in yarn on a knit stitch, insert the right-hand needle into the next stitch and lay the yarn to be woven in over the right-hand needle. Knit the stitch with the working yarn, taking it under the yarn not in use and making sure you do not catch this strand into the knitted stitch.

2 Knit the next stitch with the working yarn, taking it over the yarn being woven in. Continue like this, weaving the loose color over and under the working yarn alternately with each stitch until you need to use it again.

1 To weave in yarn on a purl stitch, insert the right-hand needle into the next stitch and lay the yarn to be woven in over the right-hand needle. Purl the stitch with the working yarn, taking it under the yarn not in use and making sure you do not catch this strand into the purled stitch.

2 Purl the next stitch with the working yarn, taking it over the yarn being woven in. Continue like this, weaving the loose color over and under the working yarn alternately with each stitch until you need to use it again.

seams

When you have completed the pieces of your knitting, you reach one of the most important stages. The way you sew together or finish your project determines how good your finished garment will look. There are different types of seam techniques but the best by far is mattress or ladder stitch, which creates an invisible seam. It can be used on stockinette stitch, ribbing, garter stitch, and seed stitch.

The seam that I use for almost all sewing up is mattress stitch, which produces a wonderful invisible seam. It works well on any yarn, and makes a completely straight seam, as the same amount is taken up on each side. This also means that the knitted pieces should not need to be pinned together first. It is always worked on the right side of the fabric and is particularly useful for sewing seams on stripes and Fair Isle.

I use other types of seams less frequently, but they do have their uses. For instance, backstitch can sometimes be useful for sewing in a sleeve cap, to neatly ease in the fullness. It is also good for catching in loose strands of yarn on colorwork seams, where there can be a lot of short ends along the selvage. Just remember when using backstitch on your knitting that it is important to ensure that you work in a completely straight line.

The seam for joining two bound-off edges is handy for shoulder seams, while the seam for joining a bound-off edge with a side edge (selvage) is usually used when sewing a sleeve onto the body on a dropped shoulder style.

It is best to leave a long tail at the casting-on stage to use for seams on your knitting, so that the seam yarn is already secured in place. If this is not possible, when first securing the thread for the seam, you should leave a length that can be darned in afterward. All seams on knitting should be sewn with a large blunt-ended yarn or tapestry needle to avoid splitting the yarn.

Before sewing side seams, join the shoulder seams and attach the sleeves, unless they are set-in sleeves. If there are any embellishments, such as applied pockets or embroidery, this is the time to put them on, when you can lay the garment out flat.

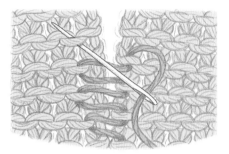

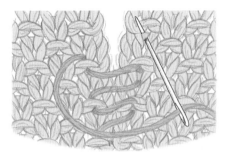

mattress stitch on stockinette stitch and double rib

With the right sides of the knitting facing you, insert the needle under the horizontal bar between the first stitch and next stitch. Then insert the needle under the same bar on the other piece. Continue to do this, drawing up the thread to form the seam.

mattress stitch on garter stitch

With the right sides of the knitting facing you, insert the needle through the bottom of the "knot" on the edge and then through the top of the corresponding "knot" on the opposite edge. Continue to do this from edge to edge, drawing up the thread to form a flat seam.

mattress stitch on seed stitch

With the right sides of the knitting facing you, insert the needle under the horizontal bar between the first and second stitches on one side and through the top of the "knot" on the edge of the opposite side.

37

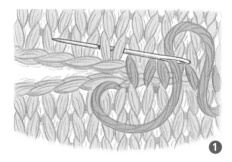

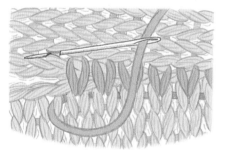

Joining two bound-off edges (grafting)

1 With the bound-off edges butted together, bring the needle out in the center of the first stitch just below the bound-off edge on one piece. Insert the needle through the center of the first stitch on the other piece and out through the center of the next stitch.

2 Next, insert the needle through the center of the first stitch on the first piece again and out through the center of the stitch next to it. Continue in this way until the seam is completed.

Joining bound-off and selvage edges

Bring the needle back to front through the center of the first stitch on the bound-off edge. Then insert it under one or two horizontal strands between the first and second stitches on the selvage and back through the center of the same bound-off stitch. Continue in this way until the seam is completed.

pickingupstitches

When you are adding a border to your garment, such as front bands or a neckband, you usually pick up stitches around the edge. A border can be sewn on afterward but this method is much neater. If you are picking up stitches along a long edge, a front band of a jacket for example, a long circular needle can be used so that you can fit all the stitches on. The pattern will usually tell you how many stitches to pick up.

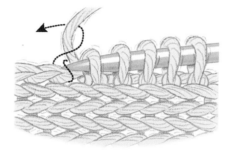

Picking up stitches along a selvage
With the right side of the knitting facing, insert the knitting needle from front to back between the first and second stitches of the first row. Wrap the yarn around the needle and pull a loop through to a form a new stitch on the needle. Continue in this way along the edge of the knitting.

Picking up stitches along a neck edge
On a neck edge, work along the straight edges as for a selvage. But along the curved edges, insert the needle through the center of the stitch below the shaping (to avoid large gaps) and pull a loop of yarn through to form a new stitch on the needle.

knitting in the round

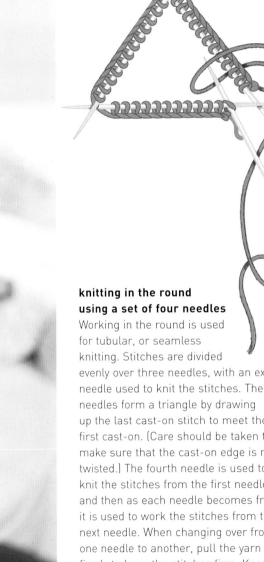

knitting in the round
using a set of four needles

Working in the round is used for tubular, or seamless knitting. Stitches are divided evenly over three needles, with an extra needle used to knit the stitches. The needles form a triangle by drawing up the last cast-on stitch to meet the first cast-on. (Care should be taken to make sure that the cast-on edge is not twisted.) The fourth needle is used to knit the stitches from the first needle, and then as each needle becomes free, it is used to work the stitches from the next needle. When changing over from one needle to another, pull the yarn firmly to keep the stitches firm. Keep track of the beginning of the round with a marker.

embroidery

Embellishing with embroidery is a great way to enhance a simple jacket such as the Daisy Cardigan or to create a particular effect as in the Baby Blanket. For those who may be unsure of their skill with Fair Isle or intarsia, embroidery is a good alternative technique for adding color to a garment.

blanket stitch

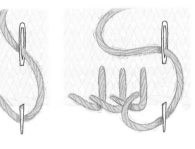

french knots

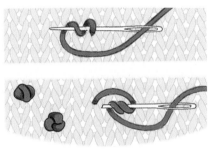

couching

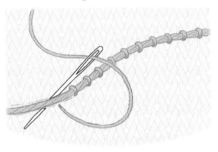

Although blanket stitch is usually used on the edge of a piece of knitting, the principle is the same for the eyelet detail on the Daisy Cardigan (see page 120). Secure the yarn to the edge of the fabric. After deciding on the height of the stitches you require and also the distance apart, insert the needle from front to back taking these requirements into account and making sure the yarn is under the needle tip at the edge of the fabric. Pull the yarn through, then re-insert the needle a short distance away, with the yarn once again under the needle. Repeat this until you have worked around the eyelet or along the edge. Fasten off, making sure the last stitch is secure.

Bring the needle up and through the fabric. Wrap the yarn twice around it, holding the thread tautly. Re-insert the needle back through the fabric as close as possible to where it emerged, pulling the yarn to hold the wraps tight.

Place the yarn on the fabric following the outline. Using matching thread to "couch," bring this thread through the fabric and over the yarn, then re-insert the needle as close as possible to where it emerged. Repeat along the length of the yarn to hold it in place. The more couching stitches you make, the more secure the yarn line will be.

pompons

Pompons are easy to create and good for decorative details on hats, scarves, and cords. Children love to make them, and they are a great way to introduce them to yarn before they learn to knit. For safety reasons, make sure that the pompon is tightly bound so that it cannot pull apart or disintegrate.

1 Cut two identical circles of cardboard that are slightly smaller than the size of the pompon you need. Cut a hole in the center of each one and hold the circles together. Thread a darning needle with yarn and wind it continually through the center and outer edges until the hole has closed.

2 Insert the tips of the scissors between the two circles and cut between and around the circles.

3 Tie a piece of yarn tightly between the two circles, and remove the cardboard.

patterns

striped sweater

sizes and measurements

To fit ages 3–6 (6–9: 9–12) months

knitted measurements

Chest 19³/₄ (20³/₄: 23¹/₄)in

Length to shoulder 9¹/₂ (10¹/₄: 11)in

Sleeve length 6¹/₄ (7: 7³/₄)in

materials

2 (3: 3) x 1³/₄oz/50g balls Debbie Bliss Cotton Cashmere in green (A) and 2 (2: 3) balls in ecru (B)

Pair each of sizes 3 and 5 knitting needles

6 small buttons

gauge

22 sts and 30 rows to 4in square over St st using size 5 needles

abbreviations

See page 27.

front

With size 3 needles and A, cast on 57 (61: 67) sts.

K 5 rows.

Change to size 5 needles.

Next row (right side) K4A, k49 (53: 59)B, k4A.

Next row K4A, p49 (53: 59)A, k4A.

Next row K all sts in A.

Next row K4A, p49 (53: 59)B, k4A.
Next row K4A, k49 (53: 59)B, k4A.
Next row (wrong side) P all sts in B.
Beg with a k row, work in St st in stripe sequence of 2 rows A and 2 rows B.
Cont until work measures 8¼ (9: 9¾)in from cast-on edge, ending with a wrong side row.
Keeping the stripe sequence correct, work as foll:
Shape neck
Next row (right side) K17 (18: 20), turn and cont on these sts only for first side of neck.
Work ¾in in stripes, ending with a wrong side row.
Buttonhole shoulder band
Change to size 3 needles and A.
K 2 rows.
Buttonhole row (right side) K4 (5: 5), yo, k2tog, k5 (5: 6), yo, k2tog, k4 (4: 5).
K 2 rows.
Bind off knitwise.
With right side facing, slip 23 (25: 27) sts at center front onto a holder, rejoin correct yarn, and knit to end.
Complete to match first side, working buttonhole row as foll:
Buttonhole row (right side) K4 (4: 5), k2tog, yo, k5 (5: 6), k2tog, yo, k4 (5: 5).

back

Work as given for Front, omitting buttonholes on shoulder bands.

sleeves

With size 3 needles and A, cast on 35 (37: 39) sts.
K 5 rows.
Change to size 5 needles.
Beg with a k row in B, work in St st in stripe sequence as foll:
2 rows B.
2 rows A.
But **at the same time**, inc 1 st at each end of the 7th row and every foll 8th row until there are 43 (47: 51) sts.
Work even until sleeve measures 6¼ (7: 7¾)in from cast-on edge, ending with a right side row.
Bind off.

neckband

With right side facing, size 3 needles, and A, pick up and k 8 sts down left front neck, k across 23 (25: 27) sts at center front, pick up and k 8 sts up right front neck. **39 (41: 43) sts.**
K 1 row.
Buttonhole row K2, yo, k2tog, k2, skp, k2tog, k19 (21: 23), skp, k2tog, k3, yo, k2tog, k1.
K 1 row.
Next row K5, skp, k2tog, k17 (19: 21), skp, k2tog, k5.
Bind off knitwise, dec at corners as before.
Work back neckband in the same way, omitting buttonholes but working corner decreases.

finishing

Lap buttonhole band over button band at shoulders and sew together at side edges. Matching center of bound-off edge of sleeve to center of shoulder bands, sew on sleeves.
Starting at top side of side splits, sew side seams. Then sew sleeve seams. Sew on buttons.

sizes and measurements
To fit ages 3–6 (6–9: 9–12: 12–18: 18–24) months
knitted measurements
Chest 20 (20³/₄: 23¹/₂: 25: 27¹/₄)in
Length to shoulder 9¹/₂ (10³/₄: 11¹/₂: 12¹/₄: 13)in
Sleeve length 5 (6: 6³/₄: 8: 8³/₄)in

materials
2 (3: 3: 4: 4) x 1³/₄oz/50g balls of Debbie Bliss Cashmerino Aran in pale pink
Long circular and pair of size 8 knitting needles
Long circular and pair of size 7 knitting needles

gauge
18 sts and 24 rows to 4in square over St st using size 8 needles.

abbreviations
See page 27.

back, front, & sleeves

Work in one piece.
With size 8 needles, cast on 8 sts.
P 1 row.
Beg with a k row, work in St st.
Cast on 10 (11: 12: 13: 14) sts at beg of next 4 rows. **48 (52: 56: 60: 64) sts.**
Beg with a k row, work 20 (24: 26: 30: 32) rows in St st.
Change to size 8 circular needle.

Shape sleeves
Cast on 5 (6: 7: 8: 9) sts at beg of next 8 rows. **88 (100: 112: 124: 136) sts.**
Work 18 (22: 24: 26: 28) rows more.

Divide for fronts
Next row K36 (41: 47: 52: 58) sts, leave these sts on a spare needle, bind off next 16 (18: 18: 20: 20) sts, k to end.
Cont on last set of 36 (41: 47: 52: 58) sts for left front.
Work even for 5 (5: 7: 5: 7) rows, ending at front edge.
Next row (right side) K3, M1, k to end.
Work even for 3 rows.
Rep the last 4 rows 2 (3: 3: 4: 4) times more and the inc row once more. **40 (46: 52: 58: 64) sts.**

Sleeve shaping
Bind off 5 (6: 7: 8: 9) sts at beg of next and 3 foll alt rows. **20 (22: 24: 26: 28) sts.**
Work even for 8 (10: 10: 12: 12) rows.

Shape front
Next row (right side) K1, skp, k to end.
Next row P to end.
Rep the last 2 rows 1 (2: 3: 4: 5) times more.
Next row Bind off 2 sts, k to end.
Next row P to end.
Next row Bind off 3 sts, k to end.
Next row P to end.
Next row Bind off 4 sts, k to end.
Next row P to end.
Next row Bind off 5 sts, k to end.
Next row P to end.
Leave rem 4 (5: 6: 7: 8) sts on a holder.

Right front
With wrong side facing, join yarn to rem 36 (41: 47: 52: 58) sts on spare needle, p to end.
Work even for 4 (4: 6: 4: 6) rows, ending at side edge.
Next row (right side) K to last 3 sts, M1, k3.
Work even for 3 rows.
Rep the last 4 rows 2 (3: 3: 4: 4) times more and the inc row once more. **40 (46: 52: 58: 64) sts.**
Work 1 row, so ending at sleeve edge.

Sleeve shaping
Bind off 5 (6: 7: 8: 9) sts at beg of next and 3 foll alt rows. **20 (22: 24: 26: 28) sts.**

Work even for 7 (9: 9: 11: 11) rows.
Shape front
Next row (right side) K to last 3 sts, k2tog, k1.
Next row P to end.
Rep the last 2 rows 1 (2: 3: 4: 5) times more.
Next row K to end.
Next row Bind off 2 sts, p to end.
Next row K to end.
Next row Bind off 3 sts, p to end.
Next row K to end.
Next row Bind off 4 sts, p to end.
Next row K to end.
Next row Bind off 5 sts, p to end.
Leave rem 4 (5: 6: 7: 8) sts on a holder.

front edging

With right side of lower right front facing and size 7 circular needle, k4 (5: 6: 7: 8) sts from holder, pick up and k22 (24: 26: 28: 30) sts evenly around right front to top of shaping, 11 (11: 13: 13: 15) sts along straight edge, then 16 (18: 20: 22: 24) sts to shoulder, 24 (26: 28: 30: 32) sts from back neck, 16 (18: 20: 22: 24) sts down left front to beg of neck shaping, 11 (11: 13: 13: 15) sts along straight edge, and k22 (24: 26: 28: 30) sts evenly around shaped edge, then k4 (5: 6: 7: 8) sts from holder. **130 (142: 158: 170: 186) sts.**
1st row P2, * k2, p2; rep from * to end.
2nd row K2, * p2, k2; rep from * to end.
Rep the last 2 rows once more and 1st row again.
Bind off in rib.

lower back edging

With right side facing and size 7 needles, pick up and k54 (58: 62: 66: 70) sts along lower edge of back.
Work 5 rows in rib as given for front edging.
Bind off in rib.

cuffs

With right side facing and size 7 needles, pick up and k30 (34: 42: 46: 50) sts along lower edge of sleeve.
Work 5 rows in rib as given for front edging.
Bind off in rib.

finishing

Sew side and sleeve seams.

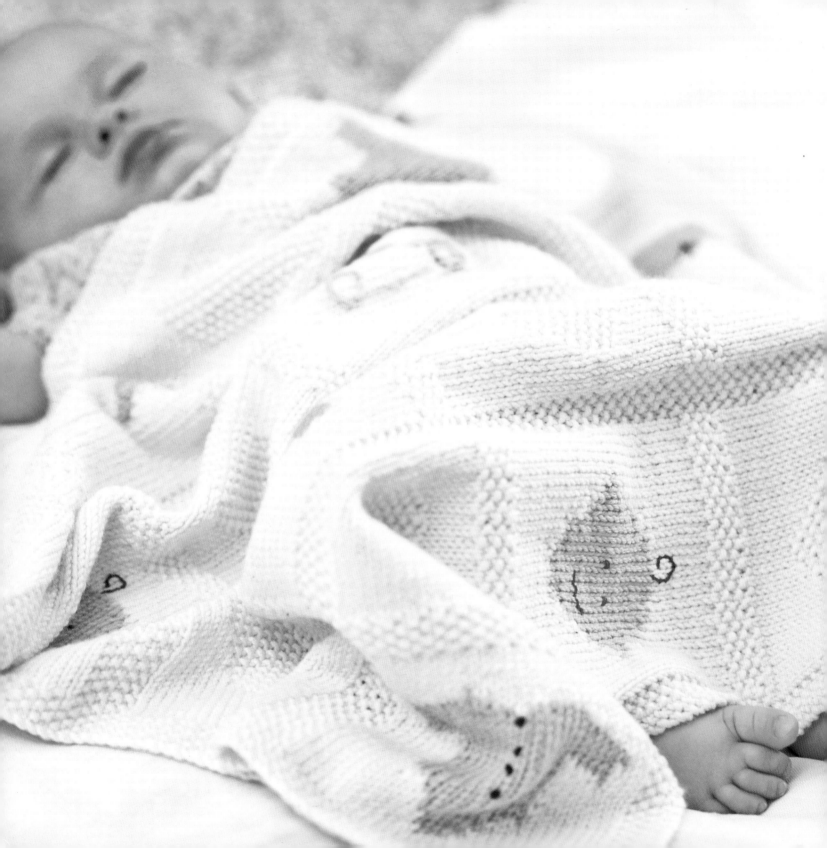

baby blanket

size
Length 23¹/₂in
Width 21¹/₄in

materials
4 x 1³/₄oz/50g balls of Debbie Bliss Baby Cashmerino in ecru (M) and 1 ball each in
pale pink (A) and pale blue (B)
Long circular or pair of long size 3 knitting needles
Brown cotton embroidery floss
Pale pink sewing thread

gauge
25 sts and 34 rows to 4in square over St st using size 3 needles.

abbreviations
See page 27.

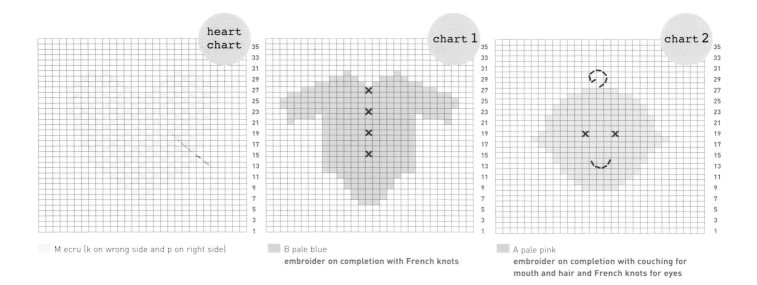

M ecru (k on wrong side and p on right side)

B pale blue
embroider on completion with French knots

A pale pink
embroider on completion with couching for mouth and hair and French knots for eyes

chart notes

All charts are worked in St st unless otherwise indicated. When working from a chart, read odd rows (k rows) from right to left, and read even rows (p rows) from left to right.

When working motifs, use the intarsia method (see pages 32–3), knitting with separate small balls of yarn for each area of color and twisting yarns on wrong side when changing color to avoid holes.

blanket

With size 3 needles and M, cast on 141 sts.
Seed st row K1, [p1, k1] to end.
Rep this row 5 times more.

First line of motifs
Next row (right side) Seed st 5, work across 29 sts of Chart 1, seed st 5, work across 29 sts of Heart Chart, seed st 5, work across 29 sts of Chart 2, seed st 5, work across 29 sts of Heart Chart, seed st 5.
Cont as set on last row for seed st and charts until all 36 rows of charts have been worked.
Work 6 rows in seed st across all sts.

Second line of motifs
Next row (right side) Seed st 5, work across 29 sts of Heart Chart, seed st 5, work across 29 sts of Chart 3, seed st 5, work across 29 sts of Heart Chart, seed st 5, work across 29 sts of Chart 4, seed st 5.
Cont as set on last row until all 36 rows of charts have been worked.
Work 6 rows in seed st across all sts.

Third line of motifs
Next row (right side) Seed st 5, work across 29 sts of Chart 2, seed st 5, work across 29 sts of

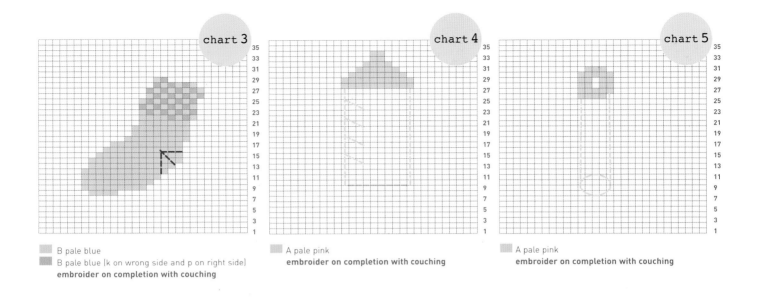

chart 3

- **B pale blue**
- **B pale blue** (k on wrong side and p on right side)
  embroider on completion with couching

chart 4

- **A pale pink**
  embroider on completion with couching

chart 5

- **A pale pink**
  embroider on completion with couching

Heart Chart, seed st 5, work across 29 sts of Chart 5, seed st 5, work across 29 sts of Heart Chart, seed st 5.

Cont as set on last row until all 36 rows of charts have been worked.

Work 6 rows in seed st across all sts.

Fourth line of motifs

Next row (right side) Seed st 5, work across 29 sts of Heart Chart, seed st 5, work across 29 sts of Chart 4, seed st 5, work across 29 sts of Heart Chart, seed st 5, work across 29 sts of Chart 1, seed st 5.

Cont as set on last row until all 36 rows of charts have been worked.

Work 6 rows in seed st across all sts.

Fifth line of motifs

Next row (right side) Seed st 5, work across 29 sts of Chart 5, seed st 5, work across 29 sts of Heart Chart, seed st 5, work across 29 sts of Chart 3, seed st 5, work across 29 sts of Heart Chart, seed st 5.

Cont as set on last row until all 36 rows of charts have been worked.

Work 5 rows in seed st across all sts.

Bind off in seed st.

finishing

Work embroidery as indicated on charts (see above). For the French knots and couched lines on Charts 1, 2, and 3, use three strands of brown stranded cotton, and use one strand for couching threads in place. For the couched lines on charts 4 and 5, use one strand of pale pink yarn (A), and couch in place with sewing thread.

crossover jacket

sizes and measurements
To fit ages 3–6 (6–9: 9–12: 12–18: 18–24) months
knitted measurements
Chest 19³/₄ (21¹/₄: 24: 25¹/₄: 27¹/₂)in
Length to shoulder 9¹/₂ (10¹/₄: 11¹/₂: 12¹/₂: 14¹/₄)in
Sleeve length 5¹/₂ (6¹/₄: 7: 8: 8³/₄)in

materials
3 (4: 4: 5: 5) x 1³/₄oz/50g balls of Debbie Bliss Cashmerino Aran in main color (M) and 1 ball in contrasting color (C)
Pair each of sizes 7 and 8 knitting needles
One button
20in of narrow ribbon or leather thonging

gauge
24 sts and 24 rows to 4in square over rib using size 8 needles

abbreviations
See page 27.

back

With size 8 needles and C, cast on 62 (66: 74: 78: 86) sts.
1st row (right side) K2, * p2, k2; rep from * to end.
2nd row P2, * k2, p2; rep from * to end.
These 2 rows form the rib.
Change to M.
Cont in rib until back measures $5^1/2$ (6: $6^3/4$: $7^1/2$: $8^3/4$)in from cast-on edge, ending with a wrong side row.
Shape armholes
Cast on 1 st at beg of next 2 rows. 64 (68: 76: 80: 88) sts.
Cont in rib until back measures $9^1/2$ ($10^1/4$: $11^1/2$: $12^1/2$: $14^1/4$)in from cast-on edge, ending with a wrong side row.
Bind off.

left front

With size 8 needles and C, cast on 40 (44: 48: 48: 52) sts.
1st row (right side) K2, * p2, k2; rep from * to last 6 sts, p2, k4.
2nd row * K2, p2; rep from * to end.
These 2 rows form the rib.
Change to M.
Cont in rib until front measures $5^1/2$ (6: $6^3/4$: $7^1/2$: $8^3/4$)in from cast-on edge, ending with a wrong side row.
Shape armhole
Cast on 1 st at beg of next row. 41 (45: 49: 49: 53) sts.
Working cast-on st as p1 on right side rows and k1 on wrong side rows, cont in rib as now set until front measures $8^3/4$ ($9^1/2$: $9^1/2$: $10^3/4$: $11^1/2$)in from cast-on edge, ending with a wrong side row.
Buttonhole row Rib to last 4 sts, k2tog, yo, k2.
Shape neck
Next row Bind off 21 (24: 27: 26: 29) sts, patt to end.
Work even in rib as set until front measures same as Back to shoulder, ending with a wrong side row.
Bind off.

right front

With size 8 needles and C, cast on 40 (44: 48: 48: 52) sts.
1st row (right side) K4, * p2, k2; rep from * to end.
2nd row P2, * k2, p2; rep from * to last 2 sts, k2.
These 2 rows form the rib.
Change to M.
Cont in rib until front measures $5^1/2$ (6: $6^3/4$: $7^1/2$: $8^3/4$)in from cast-on edge, ending with a right side row.
Shape armhole
Cast on 1 st at beg of next row. 41 (45: 49: 49: 53) sts.
Working cast on st as p1 on right side rows and k1 on wrong side rows, work even until front measures same as Back to shoulder, ending with a wrong side row.
Bind off.

sleeves

With size 8 needles and C, cast on 42 (46: 50: 54: 58) sts.
1st row (right side) K2, * p2, k2; rep from * to end.
Change to M.
2nd row P2, * k2, p2; rep from * to end.
These 2 rows form the rib.
Work 6 rows more in rib.
Change to size 7 needles.
Work 8 rows more.
Change to size 8 needles.
Cont in rib and inc 1 st at each end of the 5th and every foll 4th row until there are
52 (58: 64: 72: 76) sts.
Work even until sleeve measures 7$\frac{1}{2}$ (8$\frac{1}{4}$: 9: 10: 10$\frac{3}{4}$)in from cast-on edge, ending with a
wrong side row.
Bind off.

finishing

Sew shoulder seams. Sew on sleeves. Sew side and sleeve seams, reversing seam for 2in cuff.
Overlapping left front with right front, sew button to wrong side of right front to correspond
with buttonhole. Cut ribbon in half and sew one piece to right front edge and other piece to
left front to match, then tie.

sizes and measurements
To fit ages 3–6 (6–9: 9–12) months
knitted measurements
Chest 19³/₄ (20³/₄: 22)in
Length to shoulder 10¹/₄ (11: 11³/₄)in
Sleeve length 6 (6¹/₄: 6³/₄)in

materials
3 (4: 4) x 1³/₄oz/50g balls Debbie Bliss Baby Cashmerino in teal
Pair each of 2, 3, 5, and 6 knitting needles
1¹/₄yd of narrow ribbon

gauge
25 sts and 34 rows to 4in square over St st using size 3 needles.

abbreviations
sk2p = slip 1, k2tog, pass slipped st over.
See page 27.

note
When measuring the length from the cast-on edge, the measurement
should be taken along the length of the single st between eyelet holes.

matinee coat

back

With size 6 needles, cast on 81 (89: 97) sts.

1st row K1, * yo, k2, sk2p, k2, yo, k1; rep from * to end.

2nd row P to end.

Rep these 2 rows until back measures 2¹/₄in from cast-on edge (see Note) ending with a p row.

Change to size 5 needles and cont in patt until back measures 4¹/₄ (4³/₄: 5) in from cast-on edge, ending with a p row.

Change to size 3 needles and cont in patt until back measures 6 (6¹/₄: 6³/₄) in from cast-on edge, ending with a 1st row.

Dec row (wrong side) P10 (5: 2), p2tog, p1 (3: 1), [p2tog, p3 (1: 3), p2tog, p1 (3: 1)] 7 (9: 11) times, p2tog, p10 (5: 2). **65 (69: 73) sts.**

Beg with a k row, work in St st until back measures 10¹/₄ (11: 11³/₄) in, ending with a p row.

Shape shoulders

Bind off 20 (21: 22) sts at beg of next 2 rows.

Leave rem 25 (27: 29) sts on a holder.

left front

With size 6 needles, cast on 42 (50: 58) sts.
1st row K1, * yo, k2, sk2p, k2, yo, k1; rep from * to last st, k1.
2nd row P to end.
** Rep these 2 rows until front measures 2^1/$_4$in from cast-on edge, ending with a p row.
Change to size 5 needles and cont in patt until front measures 4^1/$_4$ (4^3/$_4$: 5) in from cast-on edge, ending with a p row.
Change to size 3 needles and cont in patt until front measures 6 (6^1/$_4$: 6^3/$_4$) in from cast-on edge, ending with a 1st row.
Dec row (wrong side) P and dec 8 (14: 20) sts evenly across row. **34 (36: 38) sts.**
K 1 row.
Shape neck
Cont in st st and bind off 2 sts at beg (neck edge) of next row and foll wrong side row, then dec 1 st at same edge of next 5 (6: 7) alt rows, then on every foll 4th row until 20 (21: 22) sts rem.
Work even until front measures same as Back to shoulder.
Bind off.

right front

With size 6 needles, cast on 42 (50: 58) sts.
1st row K2, * yo, k2, sk2p, k2, yo, k1: rep from * to end.
2nd row P to end.
Work exactly as for Left Front from ** to **.
Shape neck
Bind off 2 sts at (neck edge) of next row and foll right side row, then dec 1 st at same edge of next 5 (6: 7) alt rows, then on every foll 4th row until 20 (21: 22) sts rem.
Work even until front measures same as Back to shoulder.
Bind off.

sleeves

With size 6 needles, cast on 41 (41: 49) sts.
1st row K1, * yo, k2, sk2p, k2, yo, k1; rep from * to end.
2nd row P to end.
Rep these 2 rows 3 times more.
Change to size 3 needles.
Beg with a k row, work in St st, **at the same time**, inc 1 st at each end of the 5th row and 6 (9: 8) foll 5th (4th: 5th) rows. **55 (61: 67) sts.**
Work even until sleeve measures 6 (6^1/$_4$: 6^3/$_4$) in, ending with a p row.
Bind off.

edgings

Sew shoulder seams.
With right side facing and size 2 needles, pick up and k 44 (46: 48) sts up right front edge to start of neck shaping, 26 (28: 32) sts to shoulder, 25 (27: 29) sts across back neck, 26 (28: 32) sts down left front neck, then 44 (46: 48) sts down left front edge. **165 (175: 189) sts.**
Bind off knitwise.

finishing

Matching center of bound-off edge of sleeve to shoulder, sew on sleeves. Sew side and sleeve seams. Thread ribbon around back and front through last eyelet row before yoke, to tie at front.

teddy bear

• • • • • • • • • • • •

size
Approximately 12in tall

materials
2 x $1^3/_4$oz/50g balls Debbie Bliss Baby Cashmerino in stone
Pair of size 3 knitting needles
Washable toy filling
Black felt and matching sewing thread

gauge
27 sts and 56 rows to 4in square over garter st
using size 3 needles

abbreviations
kfb = k into front and back of next st.
sk2p = slip 1, k2tog, pass slipped st over.
See page 27.

body

Make 2 pieces, beg at shoulders.
With size 3 needles, cast on 22 sts.
K 10 rows.
Cont in garter st and inc 1 st at each end of next row and 6 foll 6th rows. **36 sts.**
K 7 rows.
Shape base
Next row K1, skp, k13, k2tog, skp, k13, k2tog, k1. **32 sts.** K 1 row.
Next row K1, skp, k11, k2tog, skp, k11, k2tog, k1. **28 sts.** K 1 row.
Next row K1, skp, k9, k2tog, skp, k9, k2tog, k1. **24 sts.** K 1 row.
Cont to dec 4 sts on every alt row in this way until 8 sts rem. K 1 row.
Next row K1, sk2p, k3tog, k1. **4 sts.**
Next row [K2tog] twice.
Next row K2tog and fasten off.

head

Make 1 piece.
With size 3 needles, cast on 32 sts. K 2 rows.
Next row [Kfb, k6, kfb] 4 times. **40 sts.** K 1 row.
Next row [Kfb, k8, kfb] 4 times. **48 sts.** K 1 row.
Next row [Kfb, k10, kfb] 4 times. **56 sts.** K 30 rows.
Shape top
Next row [Skp, k10, k2tog] 4 times. **48 sts.** K 1 row.
Next row [Skp, k8, k2tog] 4 times. **40 sts.** K 1 row.
Next row [Skp, k6, k2tog] 4 times. **32 sts.** K 1 row.
Next row [Skp, k4, k2tog] 4 times. **24 sts.** K 1 row.
Next row [Skp, k2, k2tog] 4 times. **16 sts.** K 1 row.
Next row [Skp, k2tog] 4 times. **8 sts.** K 1 row.
Next row [Skp, k2tog] twice. **4 sts.**
Break off yarn, thread through rem sts, pull to gather, and secure.

snout

Make 1 piece.
With size 3 needles, cast on 36 sts. K 10 rows.
Next row *K1, k2tog; rep from * to end. **24 sts.** K 1 row.
Next row [K2tog] to end. **12 sts.** K 1 row.
Break off yarn, thread through sts, pull to gather, and secure.

legs

Make 2 pieces.
With size 3 needles, cast on 8 sts. K 20 rows for the sole.
Shape foot
Cont in garter st and cast on 14 sts at beg of next 2 rows. **36 sts.** K 6 rows.
Dec 1 st at beg of next 10 rows. **26 sts.** K 30 rows.
Shape top
Next row K5, skp, k2tog, k8, skp, k2tog, k5. **22 sts.** K 1 row.
Next row K4, skp, k2tog, k6, skp, k2tog, k4. **18 sts.** K 1 row.
Next row K3, skp, k2tog, k4, skp, k2tog, k3. **14 sts.** K 1 row.

Next row K2, skp, k2tog, k2, skp, k2tog, k2. **10 sts.** K 1 row.
Next row K1, skp, k2tog, skp, k2tog, k1. **6 sts.**
Next row [K2tog] 3 times.
Next row K3tog and fasten off.

arms

Make 2 pieces.
With size 3 needles, cast on 4 sts. K 1 row.
Next row [Kfb] 3 times, k1. **7 sts.** K 1 row.
Next row [Kfb] 6 times, k1. **13 sts.** K 1 row.
Next row [Kfb] 12 times, k1. **25 sts.** K 36 rows.
Shape top
Next row K2tog tbl, k8, k2tog, k1, k2tog tbl, k8, k2tog. **21 sts.** K 1 row.
Next row K2tog tbl, k6, k2tog, k1, k2tog tbl, k6, k2tog. **17 sts.** K 1 row.
Next row K2tog tbl, k4, k2tog, k1, k2tog tbl, k4, k2tog. **13 sts.** K 1 row.
Next row K2tog tbl, k2, k2tog, k1, k2tog tbl, k2, k2tog. **9 sts.** K 1 row.
Next row K2tog tbl, k2tog, k1, k2tog tbl, k2tog. **5 sts.** K 1 row.
Next row K2tog tbl, k1, k2tog. **3 sts.**
Next row K3tog and fasten off.

ears

Make 2 pieces.
With size 3 needles, cast on 13 sts. K 4 rows.
Dec 1 st at each end of next row and 3 foll alt rows. **5 sts.** K 1 row.
Inc 1 st at each end of next row and 3 foll alt rows. **13 sts.** K 4 rows.
Bind off.

finishing

Sew two body pieces together, leaving cast-on edges (shoulders) open. Evenly fill with toy filling, then sew seam. Sew back seam in head, leaving neck (cast-on edge) open. Evenly fill with stuffing. Sew snout seam, leaving cast-on edge open. Position and sew to head, filling lightly. Sew base of head to shoulders. Fold each ear in half and sew to head. Sew front seam of each leg, then sew sole in place, so leaving top of leg open. Evenly fill each leg with toy filling and sew to body. Sew each arm seam, leaving top open. Evenly fill each arm with toy filling and sew to body. Cut two small circles from black felt for eyes and one quarter circle for the nose, then sew in place.

cuff bootees

sizes
To fit ages 0–3 (3–6) months

materials
1 x 1³/₄oz/50g ball of Debbie Bliss Baby Cashmerino in main color (M) and small amount in contrasting color (C)
Pair each of sizes 2 and 3 knitting needles

gauge
27 sts and 36 rows to 4in square over St st using size 3 needles.

abbreviations
See page 27.

to make

With size 2 needles and M, cast on 26 sts.
1st row K to end.
2nd row K1, yo, k11, yo, k2, yo, k11, yo, k1.
3rd and every foll alt row K to end.
4th row K2, yo, k11, yo, k4, yo, k11, yo, k2.
6th row K3, yo, k11, yo, k6, yo, k11, yo, k3.
8th row K4, yo, k11, yo, k8, yo, k11, yo, k4.
10th row K5, yo, k11, yo, k10, yo, k11, yo, k5. **46 sts.**
12th row K6, yo, k11, yo, k12, yo, k11, yo, k6. **50 sts.**
13th row K to end.
2nd size only
14th row K7, yo, k11, yo, k14, yo, k11, yo, k7. **54 sts.**
15th row K to end.
Both sizes
Change to size 3 needles.

With C, k 2 rows.

Change to M.

Next row (right side) K to end.

Next row [K1, p1] 11 (12) times, k6, [p1, k1] 11 (12) times.

The last row forms the seed st with garter st instep and is repeated twice more.

Shape instep

Keeping seed st correct, work as foll:

1st row (right side) Seed st 21 (23), k2tog, k4, k2tog, seed st 21 (23).

2nd row Seed st 21 (23), k6, seed st 21 (23).

3rd row Seed st 20 (22), k2tog, k4, k2tog, seed st 20 (22).

4th row Seed st 20 (22), k6, seed st 20 (22).

5th row Seed st 19 (21), k2tog, k4, k2tog, seed st 19 (21).

6th row Seed st 19 (21), k6, seed st 19 (21).

Cont in this way to dec 2 sts on every right side row until 28 (30) sts rem, ending with a wrong side row.

Change to size 2 needles.

Work even for 10 rows.

Place a marker at each end of last row.

Change to size 3 needles.

Next row [K1, p1] 7 times, k0 (1), turn and work on these sts.

Work 10 rows more in seed st.

Change to C.

K 2 rows.

Bind off.

With right side facing, size 3 needles, and M, rejoin yarn to rem sts and work as foll:

Next row K0 (1), [p1, k1] 7 times.

Work 10 rows more in seed st.

Change to C.

K 2 rows.

Bind off.

finishing

Sew sole and back seam to markers, then reverse seam to allow the cuff to fold onto right side.

cable yoke jacket

sizes and measurements
To fit ages 9–12 (12–18: 18–24) months
knitted measurements
Chest 25^1/$_2$ (27^1/$_4$: 29^1/$_2$)in
Length to shoulder 11^3/$_4$ (13^1/$_2$: 15)in
Sleeve length 6^1/$_4$ (7: 9)in

materials
6 (7: 8) x 1^3/$_4$oz/50g balls Debbie Bliss Cotton Double Knitting in duck egg
Pair each of sizes 5 and 6 knitting needles
Cable needle
10 (10: 12)in open-ended zipper

gauge
20 sts and 28 rows to 4in square over St st using size 6 needles.

abbreviations
C4F = slip next 2 sts onto cable needle and hold at front of work, k2, then k2 from cable needle.
pfb = purl into front and back of next st.
See page 27.

cableyoke jacket

back

With size 5 needles, cast on 67 (71: 77) sts.
Seed st row K1, [p1, k1] to end.
Rep this row 3 times more.
Change to size 6 needles.
Beg with a k row, work in St st until Back measures 6$^1/_4$ (7: 7$^3/_4$)in from cast-on edge, ending with a k row.
Inc row P3 (5: 8), [pfb, p5] 10 times, pfb, p3 (5: 8). **78 (82: 88) sts.**
Yoke
1st row (right side) Seed st 2 (4: 7), [C4F, seed st 3] 10 times, c4f, seed st 2 (4: 7).
2nd row Seed st 2 (4: 7), [p4, seed st 3] 10 times, p4, seed st 2 (4: 7).
3rd row Seed st 2 (4: 7), [k4, seed st 3] 10 times, k4, seed st 2 (4: 7).
4th row Rep 2nd row.
Rep the last 4 rows until work measures 11$^3/_4$ (13$^1/_2$: 15)in from cast-on edge, ending with a wrong side row.
Bind off all sts, working skp across center 2 sts of each cable.

left front

With size 5 needles, cast on 32 (34: 36) sts.
1st seed st row [P1, k1] to end.
2nd seed st row [K1, p1] to end.
Rep these 2 rows once more.
Change to size 6 needles and work as foll:
1st row K to last 3 sts, seed st 3.
2nd row Seed st 3, p to end.
Rep the last 2 rows until work measures 6$^1/_4$ (7: 7$^3/_4$)in from cast-on edge, ending with a right side row.
Inc row Seed st 3, p1, [pfb, p5] 4 times, pfb, p3 (5: 7) and inc 1 st in last st of 3rd size only.
37 (39: 42) sts.
Yoke
1st row (right side) Seed st 2 (4: 7), [C4F, seed st 3] 5 times.
2nd row Seed st 3, [p4, seed st 3] 4 times, p4, seed st 2 (4: 7).
3rd row Seed st 2 (4: 7), [k4, seed st 3] 5 times.
4th row Rep 2nd row.
Rep the last 4 rows until front measures 9$^3/_4$ (11: 12$^1/_2$)in, ending with a wrong side row.
Shape neck
Next row Patt 34 (36: 39) and slip rem 3 sts onto a safety pin for collar.
Next row (wrong side) Bind off the 4 sts of cable working p2tog tbl on center 2 sts, patt to end.
Patt 1 row.
Next row Bind off 3 sts, patt to end.
Now dec 1 st at neck edge on next 5 rows. **22 (24: 27) sts.**
Work a few rows in patt until front measures 11$^3/_4$ (13$^1/_2$: 15)in, ending with a wrong side row.
Bind off all sts, working skp across center 2 sts of each cable.

right front

With size 5 needles, cast on 32 (34: 36) sts.
1st seed st row [K1, p1] to end.
2nd seed st row [P1, k1] to end.
Rep these 2 rows once more.
Change to size 6 needles and work as foll:
1st row Seed st 3, k to end.
2nd row P to last 3 sts, seed st 3.
Rep the last 2 rows until front measures 6$\frac{1}{4}$ (7: 7$\frac{3}{4}$)in from cast-on edge, ending with a right side row.
1st and 2nd sizes only
Inc row P3 (5), [pfb, p5] 4 times, pfb, p1, seed st 3. **37 (39) sts.**
3rd size only
Inc row Inc in first st, p6, [pfb, p5] 4 times, pfb, p1, seed st 3. **42 sts.**
All sizes
Yoke
1st row (right side) [Seed st 3, C4F] 5 times, seed st 2 (4: 7).
2nd row Seed st 2 (4: 7), [p4, seed st 3] 5 times.
3rd row [Seed st 3, k4] 5 times, seed st 2 (4: 7).
4th row Rep 2nd row.
Rep the last 4 rows until front measures 9$\frac{3}{4}$ (11: 12$\frac{1}{2}$)in, ending with a wrong side row.
Shape neck
Next row Seed st 3 and slip these sts onto a safety pin for collar, bind off next 4 sts of cable working skp on center 2 sts, then patt to end.
Patt 1 row.
Next row Bind off 3 sts, patt to end.
Patt 1 row, then dec 1 st at neck edge of next 5 rows. **22 (24: 27) sts.**
Work a few rows in patt until work measures 11$\frac{3}{4}$ (13$\frac{1}{2}$: 15)in, ending with a wrong side row.
Bind off all sts, working skp across center 2 sts of each cable.

sleeves

With size 5 needles, cast on 31 (33: 35) sts.
Seed st row K1, [p1, k1] to end.
Rep this row 3 times more.
Inc row (right side) K all sts and inc 4 (4: 6) sts evenly across row. **35 (37: 41) sts.**
Change to size 6 needles.
Beg with a p row, work in St st and inc 1 st at each end of 4th (4th: 2nd) and every foll 4th (4th: 6th) row until there are 51 (55: 59) sts.
Work even until sleeve measures 6$\frac{1}{4}$ (7: 9)in from cast-on edge, ending with a p row.
Bind off.

collar

Sew shoulder seams.
With right side facing and size 5 needles, slip 3 sts from right front safety pin onto needle, join on yarn and pick up and k 15 (16: 17) sts up right front neck, 29 (31: 33) sts across back neck, 15 (16: 17) sts down left front neck, then seed st across 3 sts from left front safety pin. **65 (69: 73) sts.**
Seed st 1 row as set by sts from safety pins.
Next 2 rows Seed st to last 21 sts, turn.
Next 2 rows Seed st to last 16 sts, turn.
Next 2 rows Seed st to last 11 sts, turn.
Next 2 rows Seed st to last 6 sts, turn.
Next row Seed st across all sts.
Seed st 10 rows.
Bind off in seed st.

finishing

With center of bound-off edge of sleeve to shoulder, sew on sleeves. Sew side and sleeve seams. Hand-sew zipper to fronts with zipper tape behind seed st edge.

smock coat

sizes and measurements
To fit ages 3–6 (6–12: 12–18: 24–36) months
knitted measurements
Chest 23$\frac{1}{2}$ (25$\frac{1}{2}$: 26$\frac{3}{4}$: 28)in
Length 14$\frac{1}{4}$ (15$\frac{1}{4}$: 17: 19$\frac{3}{4}$)in
Sleeve seam 6$\frac{1}{4}$ (7: 8: 9)in

materials
8 (8: 9: 10) x 1$\frac{3}{4}$oz/50g balls of Debbie Bliss Cotton Cashmere in chocolate brown
Pair each of sizes 3 and 5 knitting needles
4 (4: 4: 6) buttons
1$\frac{1}{4}$yd of $\frac{1}{2}$in wide velvet ribbon

gauge
22 sts and 36 rows to 4in square over seed st on size 5 needles.

abbreviations
See page 27.

back

With size 3 needles, cast on 103 (109: 115: 121) sts.
K 3 rows.
Change to size 5 needles.
Next row P1, * k1, p1; rep from * to end.
This row forms the seed st.
Cont in seed st until back measures 8$\frac{1}{4}$ (9: 10$\frac{1}{4}$: 12$\frac{1}{2}$)in from cast-on edge, ending with a wrong side row.
Dec row Seed st 2, * work 3 tog, seed st 3; rep from * to last 5 sts, work 3 tog, seed st 2.
69 (73: 77: 81)sts
Change to size 3 needles.
Cont in seed st until back measures 10$\frac{1}{4}$ (11: 12$\frac{1}{4}$: 14$\frac{1}{2}$)in from cast-on edge, ending with a wrong side row.
Shape armholes
Bind off 5 (6: 7: 8) sts at beg of next 2 rows. **59 (61: 63: 65) sts.**
Work even until back measures 14$\frac{1}{4}$ (15$\frac{1}{4}$: 17: 19$\frac{3}{4}$)in from cast-on edge, ending with a wrong side row.
Shape shoulders
Bind off 10 sts at beg of next 2 rows and 10 (10: 10: 11) sts at beg of foll 2 rows.
Bind off rem 19 (21: 23: 23) sts.

left front

With size 3 needles, cast on 57 (59: 65: 67) sts.
K 3 rows.
Change to size 5 needles.
Next row (right side) * K1, p1; rep from * to last 3 sts, k3.
Next row K3, * p1, k1; rep from * to end.
These 2 rows set the seed st with garter st border.
Cont in patt until front measures 8$\frac{1}{4}$ (9: 10$\frac{1}{4}$: 12$\frac{1}{2}$)in from cast-on edge, ending with a wrong side row.
Dec row Seed st 3, [work 3 tog, seed st 3] 6 (6: 7: 7) times, seed st to last 3 sts, k3.
45 (47: 51: 53) sts.
Change to size 3 needles.
Cont in seed st until front measures 10$\frac{1}{4}$ (11: 12$\frac{1}{4}$: 14$\frac{1}{2}$)in from cast-on edge, ending with a wrong side row.
Shape armhole
Bind off 5 (6: 7: 8) sts at beg of next row. **40 (41: 44: 45) sts.**
Work even until front measures 10$\frac{3}{4}$ (11$\frac{1}{2}$: 13: 15$\frac{3}{4}$)in from cast-on edge, ending with a wrong side row.
Shape neck
Next row (right side) Seed st to last 3 sts, turn and leave these 3 sts on a safety pin for left collar.
Dec 1 st at neck edge on every row until 20 (20: 20: 21) sts rem.
Work even until front measures same as Back to shoulder, ending at side edge.
Shape shoulder
Bind off 10 sts at beg of next row.
Work 1 row.
Bind off rem 10 (10: 10: 11) sts.
Mark positions for buttons, the first pair level with first row of seed st yoke, the 2nd (2nd: 2nd: 3rd) pair $\frac{1}{2}$in below neck shaping, and the remaining 0 (0: 0: 1) pair spaced evenly between.

right front

With size 3 needles, cast on 57 (59: 65: 67) sts.
K 3 rows.
Change to size 5 needles.
Next row (right side) K3, * p1, k1; rep from * to end.
Next row * K1, p1; rep from * to last 3 sts, k3.
These 2 rows set the seed st with garter st border.
Cont in patt until front measures 8^1/$_4$ (9: 10^1/$_4$: 12^1/$_2$)in from cast-on edge, ending with a wrong side row.
Next row K3, yo, work 2 tog, seed 10 (12: 12: 14), work 2 tog, yo, seed st 2, turn and cont on these 19 (21: 21: 23) sts only.
Work 6 rows more (for vertical slot) on these sts.
Leave these sts on a spare needle.
With right side facing, rejoin yarn to rem 38 (38: 44: 44) sts and work as foll:
Next row [Work 3 tog, seed st 3] 6 (6: 7: 7) times, seed st 2. **26 (26: 30: 30) sts.**
Work 6 rows more in seed st on these sts.
Next row (wrong side) Seed to end, then seed st across sts on spare needle. **45 (47: 51: 53) sts.**
Working 1 (1: 1: 2) more pairs of buttonholes to match markers, cont as foll:
Cont in seed st until front measures 10^1/$_4$ (11: 12^1/$_4$: 14^1/$_2$)in from cast-on edge, ending with a right side row.
Shape armhole
Bind off 5 (6: 7: 8) sts at beg of next row. **40 (41: 44: 45) sts.**
Work even until front measures 10^3/$_4$ (11^1/$_2$: 13: 15^3/$_4$)in from cast on edge, ending with a wrong side row.
Shape neck
Next row (right side) K3, leave these sts on a safety pin for right collar, seed st to end.
Dec 1 st at neck edge on every row until 20 (20: 20: 21) sts rem.
Work even until front measures same as Back to shoulder, ending at side edge.
Shape shoulder
Bind off 10 sts at beg of next row.
Work 1 row.
Bind off rem 10 (10: 10: 11) sts.

sleeves

With size 3 needles, cast on 31 (33: 37: 39) sts.
K 3 rows.
Change to size 5 needles.
Next row P1, * k1, p1; rep from * to end.
This row forms the seed st.
Work 3 rows more.
Inc 1 st at each end of the next row and every foll 6th row until there are 41 (47: 55: 59) sts.
Work even until sleeve measures 6^1/$_4$ (7: 8: 9)in from cast-on edge, ending with a wrong side row.
Mark each end of last row with a colored thread.
Work 8 (10: 10: 12) rows more.
Bind off.

left collar

With right side facing and size 3 needles, k across 3 sts of left front band.
K 1 row.
Cont in garter st and inc 1 st at each end of the next row and every foll 4th row until there are 21 sts, ending at outer edge of collar.
Shape collar
** Next 2 rows K12, sl 1, turn, k to end.
K 4 rows.**
Rep from ** to ** until short edge of collar fits up left side of front neck and halfway across back neck edge.
Bind off.

right collar

With wrong side facing and size 3 needles, k across 3 sts on right front band.
Cont in garter st and inc 1 st at each end of the next row and every foll 4th row until there are 21 sts.
K 1 row, so ending at outer edge of collar.
Shape collar
** Next 2 rows K12, sl 1, turn k to end.
K 4 rows.**
Rep from ** to ** until short edge of collar fits up right front neck and halfway across back neck edge.
Bind off.

finishing

Sew shoulder seams. Sew bound-off edges of collar. Sew collar in place. Sew sleeves into armholes with row-ends above markers sewn to sts bound off at underarm. Sew side and sleeve seams. Sew on buttons. Cut ribbon in half and sew one piece to left front edge, level with vertical slot on right front and sew rem piece to right front edge to match.

sizes

To fit ages 3–6 (9–12: 18–24) months

materials

1 x 1³/₄oz/50g ball of Debbie Bliss Cashmerino Aran in duck egg blue (A) and small amount in chocolate brown (B)
Pair each of sizes 7 and 8 knitting needles

gauge

18 sts and 24 rows to 4in square over St st using size 8 needles.
20 sts and 36 rows to 4in square over garter st using size 8 needles.

pompon beret

to make

With size 7 needles and B, cast on 56 (64: 72) sts.
Rib row * K1, p1; rep from * to end.
This row forms the rib.
Change to A.
Work 5 rows more in rib.
Change to size 8 needles.
K 4 rows.
Inc row K2, * M1, k4; rep from * to last 2 sts, M1, k2. **70 (80: 90) sts.**
K 3 rows.
Inc row K2, * M1, k5; rep from * to last 3 sts, M1, k3. **84 (96: 108) sts.**
K 13 rows.
Dec row K1, * skp, k4; rep from * to last 5 sts, skp, k3. **70 (80: 90) sts.**
K 3 rows.
Dec row K1, * skp, k3; rep from * to last 4 sts, skp, k2. **56 (64: 72) sts.**
K 3 rows.
Dec row K1, * skp, k2; rep from * to last 3 sts, skp, k1. **42 (48: 54) sts.**
K 3 rows.
Dec row K1, * skp, k1; rep from * to last 2 sts, skp. **28 (32: 36) sts.**
K 3 rows.
Dec row * Skp; rep from * to end. **14 (16: 18) sts.**
K 1 row.
Dec row * Skp; rep from * to end. **7 (8: 9) sts.**
Break off yarn, thread end through rem sts, pull to gather, and secure.

finishing

Sew seam. Make a small pompon from B (see page 41) and sew to top of beret.

lace edge cardigan

sizes and measurements

To fit ages 3–6 (6–9: 9–12: 12–18: 18–24) months

knitted measurements

Chest 19³/₄ (21¹/₄: 23¹/₄: 24¹/₂: 26³/₄)in

Length to shoulder 8³/₄ (9¹/₂: 10: 11¹/₂: 12¹/₂)in

Sleeve length 4³/₄ (5¹/₂: 6¹/₄: 7: 7³/₄)in

materials

3 (4: 4: 5: 6) x 1³/₄oz/50g balls of Debbie Bliss Baby Cashmerino in pale pink

Pair of size 3 knitting needles .

gauge

26 sts and 52 rows to 4in square over garter st using size 3 needles.

abbreviations

kfb = knit into front and back of st.

See page 27.

back & fronts

Worked in one piece to armholes.
With size 3 needles, cast on 117 (127: 139: 149: 163) sts.
Work even in garter st (knit every row) until work measures $4^3/4$ (5: $5^1/2$: $6^1/4$: 7)in from cast-on edge, ending with a right side row.

Divide for back and fronts
Next row K23 (25: 28: 31: 34), these sts will form left front, bind off 6 sts for left underarm, k until there are 59 (65: 71: 75: 83) sts on right needle, these sts will form the back, bind off 6 sts for right underarm, k to end.
Cont on last set of 23 (25: 28: 31: 34) sts for right front, place rem 2 groups of sts on holders.
Next row (right side) K5, skp, k16 (18: 21: 24: 27).
K 3 rows.
Next row K5, skp, k to end.
Rep the last 4 rows until 12 (13: 15: 16: 18) sts rem.
Work even until front measures $8^3/4$ ($9^1/2$: 10: $11^1/2$: $12^1/2$)in from cast-on edge, ending with a wrong side row.
Leave sts on a holder.

Left front
With right side facing, rejoin yarn to 23 (25: 28: 31: 34) sts held on holder for left front,
k16 (18: 21: 24: 27), k2tog, k5.
K 3 rows.
Rep the last 4 rows until 12 (13: 15: 16: 18) sts rem.
Work even until front measures $8^3/4$ ($9^1/2$: 10: $11^1/2$: $12^1/2$)in from cast-on edge, ending with a wrong side row.
Leave sts on a holder.

Back
With right side facing, rejoin yarn to 59 (65: 71: 75: 83) sts held on holder for back, k to end.
Work even until back measures $8^3/4$ ($9^1/2$: 10: $11^1/2$: $12^1/2$)in from cast-on edge, ending with a wrong side row.
Leave sts on needle.

sleeves

With size 3 needles, cast on 37 (40: 45: 48: 51) sts.
K 6 rows.
Inc row Kfb, k to last 2 sts, kfb, k1.
K 5 (6: 6: 7: 8) rows.
Rep the last 6 (7: 7: 8: 9) rows, 6 (7: 7: 8: 9) times more, then the inc row once more.
53 (58: 63: 68: 73) sts.
Work even until sleeve measures $4^3/4$ ($5^1/2$: $6^1/4$: 7: $7^3/4$)in from cast-on edge.
Mark each end of last row, then k 6 rows more.
Bind off.

finishing

With wrong side facing, slip 12 (13: 15: 16: 18) sts of left front onto a size 3 needle, then with wrong side facing slip 12 (13: 15: 16: 18) sts of right front onto same needle, needle will be

pointing toward right armhole. With right sides of Fronts and Back together, bind off shoulder sts working one st of right front and one st of back together each time. When all right front sts have been bound off, cont to bind off sts of Back until 12 (13: 15: 16: 18) sts rem on left hand needle and 1 st rems on right hand needle, now bind off left front and back sts together as before.

Sew sleeve seams, leaving seam open above markers.

Sew sleeves into armholes, with bound-off edge sewn to row-ends of armhole and row-ends of sleeve sewn to bound-off sts of underarm.

edgings

With size 3 needles, cast on 5 sts.

1st row (right side) K1, yo, k2tog, yo, k2.

2nd, 4th, 6th, and 8th rows Knit.

3rd row K2, yo, k2tog, yo, k2.

5th row K3, yo, k2tog, yo, k2.

7th row K4, yo, k2tog, yo, k2.

9th row K5, yo, k2tog, yo, k2.

10th row Bind off 5 sts, k to end. **5 sts.**

These 10 rows form the lace edging and are repeated throughout.

Cuff edging (make 2)

Work reps of the 10 row patt until edging fits along lower edge of sleeve, ending with a 10th row. Bind off rem 5 sts.

Front and neck edging

Work reps of the 10 row patt until edging fits along left front edge, around back neck, and down right front edge, ending with a 10th row. Bind off rem 5 sts.

Stitch edging around front and and neck edges and around sleeve edges.

cableblanket

size
Length 31¹/₂in
Width 19³/₄in

materials
7 x 1³/₄oz/50g balls of Debbie Bliss Baby Cashmerino Double Knitting in pale blue
Sizes 3 and 6 long circular knitting needles
Cable needle

gauge
22 sts and 30 rows to 4in square over St st using size 6 needles.

abbreviations
C8B = slip next 8 sts onto cable needle and leave at back of work, k4, then k4 from cable needle.
See page 27.

to make

With size 3 circular needle, cast on 142 sts.
K 8 rows.
Inc row K6, * p4, k4, M1, k2, M1, k4; rep from * to last 10 sts, p4, k6. **160 sts.**
Change to size 6 circular needle.
1st row (right side) K4, p2, k4, * p2, k8, p2, k4; rep from * to last 6 sts, p2, k4.
2nd row K6, * p4, k2, p4, k6; rep from * to last 10 sts, p4, k6.
3rd to 6th rows Rep 1st and 2nd rows twice more.
7th row K4, p2, k4, * p2, C8B, p2, k4; rep from * to last 6 sts, p2, k4.
8th row K6, * p4, k6, p4, k2; rep from * to last 10 sts, p4, k6.
9th row K4, p2, k4, * p2, k8, p2, k4; rep from * to last 6 sts, p2, k4.
10th to 18th rows Rep rows 8th and 9th rows four times more, then the 8th row again.
19th row K4, p2, k4, * p2, C8B, p2, k4; rep from * to last 6 sts, p2, k4.
20th row K6, * p4, k2, p4, k6; rep from * to last 10 sts, p4, k6.
21st row K4, p2, k4, * p2, k8, p2, k4; rep from * to last 6 sts, p2, k4.
22nd to 24th rows Rep 20th and 21st rows once more, then the 20th row again.
These 24 rows form the patt.
Cont in patt until blanket measures approximately 30³/₄in from cast-on edge, ending with a 23rd row.
Dec row K6, * p4, k3, k2tog, k2, k2tog, k3; rep from * to last 10 sts, p4, k6. **142 sts.**
Change to size 3 circular needle.
K 8 rows.
Bind off.

sizes and measurements

To fit ages 3–6 (6–9: 9–12: 12–18: 18–24) months

knitted measurements

Chest $18^1/_2$ ($20^1/_2$: 22: 24: 26) in

Length to shoulder $8^3/_4$ ($9^1/_2$: $10^1/_4$: 11: $12^1/_2$) in

Sleeve length 5 (6: $6^3/_4$: $7^1/_2$: $8^3/_4$) in

materials

2 (3: 3: 3: 4) x $1^3/_4$oz/50g balls of Debbie Bliss Baby Cashmerino in teal (M) and 1 ball each pale blue (A), indigo (B), lime (C), burgundy (D), and ecru (E)

Pair each of sizes 2 and 3 knitting needles

One each of sizes 2 and 3 circular needles

6 (6: 6: 7: 7) buttons

gauge

25 sts and 34 rows to 4in square over St st using size 3 needles.

fair isle cardigan

back

With size 2 needles and A, cast on 61 (67: 73: 79: 85) sts.

1st rib row K1, * p1, k1; rep from * to end.

Change to M.

2nd rib row P1, * k1, p1; rep from * to end.

Rep the 2 rib rows 2 (2: 3: 3: 4) times more.

Change to size 3 needles.

Beg with a k row, work in St st until back measures $4^3/_4$ (5: $5^1/_2$: 6: $6^3/_4$) in from cast-on edge, ending with a p row.

Shape armholes

Bind off 4 sts at beg of next 2 rows. **53 (59: 65: 71: 77) sts.**

Work even until back measures $5^1/_2$ ($6^1/_4$: 7: 8: $9^1/_2$) in from cast-on edge, ending with a p row.

Shape yoke

Next row (right side) K22 (24: 26: 28: 30), turn and work on these sts.

Bind off 3 (4: 5: 6: 7) sts at beg of next row, and 2 sts at beg of 3 foll alt rows.

Now dec 1 st on every foll alt row until 6 (7: 8: 9: 10) sts rem.

Work even until back measures $8^3/_4$ ($9^1/_2$: $10^1/_4$: 11: $12^1/_2$) in from cast-on edge, ending at armhole edge.

Shape shoulder

Bind off.

With right side facing, slip center 9 (11: 13: 15: 17) sts onto a holder, rejoin yarn to rem sts, k to end.
P 1 row.
Complete to match first side.

left front

With size 2 needles and A, cast on 29 (33: 35: 37: 41) sts.
1st rib row P1, * k1, p1; rep from * to end.
Change to M.
2nd rib row K1, * p1, k1; rep from * to end.
Rep the 2 rib rows 2 (2: 3: 3: 4) times more.
Change to size 3 needles.
Beg with a k row, work in St st until front measures $4^3/_4$ (5: $5^1/_2$: 6: $6^3/_4$) in from cast-on edge, ending with a p row.
Shape armhole
Bind off 4 sts at beg of next row. **25 (29: 31: 33: 37) sts.**
Work even until front measures $5^1/_2$ ($6^1/_4$: 7: 8: $9^1/_2$) in from cast-on edge, ending with a p row.
Shape yoke
Next row (right side) K22 (24: 26: 28: 30), turn and work on these sts, leave rem 3 (5: 5: 5: 7) sts on a holder.
Bind off 3 (4: 5: 6: 7) sts at beg of next row, and 2 sts at beg of 3 foll alt rows.
Now dec 1 st at beg of every foll alt row until 6 (7: 8: 9: 10) sts rem.
Work even until front measures $8^3/_4$ ($9^1/_2$: $10^1/_4$: 11: $12^1/_2$) in from cast-on edge, ending at armhole edge.
Shape shoulder
Bind off.

right front

With size 2 needles and A, cast on 29 (33: 35: 37: 41) sts.
1st rib row P1, * k1, p1; rep from * to end.
Change to M.
2nd rib row K1, * p1, k1; rep from * to end.
Rep the 2 rib rows 2 (2: 3: 3: 4) times more.
Change to size 3 needles.
Beg with a k row, work in St st until front measures $4^3/_4$ (5: $5^1/_2$: 6: $6^3/_4$) in from cast-on edge, ending with a k row.
Shape armhole
Bind off 4 sts at beg of next row. **25 (29: 31: 33: 37) sts.**
Work even until front measures $5^1/_2$ ($6^1/_4$: 7: 8: $9^1/_2$) in from cast-on edge, ending with a p row.
Shape yoke
Next row (right side) K3 (5: 5: 5: 7) sts, leave these sts on a holder, k to end. **22 (24: 26: 28: 30) sts.**
P 1 row.
Bind off 3 (4: 5: 6: 7) sts at beg of next row, and 2 sts at beg of 3 foll alt rows.
Now dec 1 st at beg of every foll alt row until 6 (7: 8: 9: 10) sts rem.
Work even until front measures $8^3/_4$ ($9^1/_2$: $10^1/_4$: 11: $12^1/_2$) in from cast-on edge, ending at armhole edge.
Shape shoulder
Bind off.

chart notes

When working yoke from chart, work 1 edge st at beg of right side and end of wrong side rows, repeat the 12 st patt across row, then work 2 edge sts at beg of wrong side and end of right side rows. Strand and weave in yarn not in use across wrong side of work.

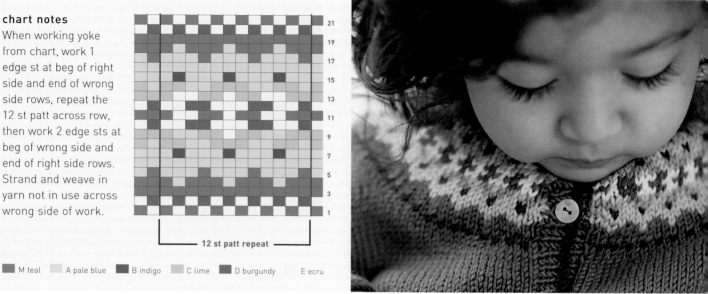

— 12 st patt repeat —

◼ M teal ◻ A pale blue ◼ B indigo ◻ C lime ◼ D burgundy ◻ E ecru

sleeves

With size 2 needles and B, cast on 32 (34: 38: 42: 46) sts.
Rib row * K1, p1; rep from * to end.
This row forms the rib.
Change to M.
Rep the rib row 5 (5: 7: 7: 9) times more.
Change to size 3 needles.
Beg with a k row, work in St st and inc 1 st at each end of the next (3rd: 5th: 3rd: 3rd) row and every foll 4th row until there are 50 (54: 58: 66: 74) sts.
Work even until sleeve measures 5 (6: 6³/₄: 7¹/₂: 8³/₄) in from cast-on edge, ending with a p row.
Mark each end of last row with a colored thread.
Work 4 rows more.
Bind off.

yoke

Sew shoulder seams.
With right side facing, size 3 circular needle, and M, slip 3 (5: 5: 5: 7) sts from right front holder onto a needle, pick up and k9 (10: 11: 12: 13) sts from bound-off sts, 13 (14: 15: 16: 17) sts to shoulder, 13 (14: 15: 16: 17) sts along row ends from shoulder to start of bound-off sts, 9 (10: 11: 12: 13) sts from bound-off sts, k9 (11: 13: 15: 17) sts from center back holder, pick up and k9 (10: 11: 12: 13) sts from bound-off sts, 13 (14: 15: 16: 17) sts to shoulder, 13 (14: 15: 16: 17) sts along row ends from shoulder to start of bound-off sts, 9 (10: 11: 12: 13) sts from bound-off sts, then k3 (5: 5: 5: 7) sts from left front holder. **103 (117: 127: 137: 151) sts.**
Next row (wrong side) P to end.

Next row (1st row of Chart) (right side) K1B, * 1E, 1B; rep from * to end.
Next row (2nd row of Chart) P1E, * 1D, 1E; rep from * to end.
Dec row (3rd row of Chart) (right side) With M, k5 (7: 3: 3: 7), [k4 (4: 6: 8: 7), k2tog] 15 (17: 15: 13: 15) times, k2tog, k6 (6: 2: 2: 7). **87 (99: 111: 123: 135) sts.**
Work 4th to 10th row from Chart.
Work 11th to 18th row from Chart.
Dec row (19th row of Chart) (right side) With M, k3, * k2tog, k5, k2tog, k3; rep from * to end. **73 (83: 93: 103: 113) sts.**
Work 2nd then 1st rows from Chart as before.
Cont in M only.
P 1 row.
K 1 row.
Dec row (wrong side) P3 * p2tog, p3; rep from * to end. **59 (67: 75: 83: 91) sts.**
K 1 row.
P 1 row.
Change to size 2 needles.
1st rib row K1, * p1, k1; rep from * to end.
2nd rib row P1, * k1, p1; rep from * to end.
3rd rib row K1, * p1, k1; rep from * to end.
Change to A.
4th rib row P1, * k1, p1; rep from * to end.
Bind off in rib.

button band

With right side facing, size 2 needles, and M, pick up and k55 (61: 67: 75: 91) sts along left front edge.
Work 3 rows in rib as given for Back.
Change to B.
Rib 1 row.
Bind off in rib.

buttonhole band

With right side facing, size 2 needles, and M, pick up and k55 (61: 67: 75: 91) sts along right front edge.
Work 1 row in rib as given for Back.
Buttonhole row (right side) Rib 2 (2: 2: 3: 2), [rib 2tog, yo, rib 8 (9: 10: 9: 12) sts] 5 (5: 5: 6: 6) times, rib 2tog, yo, rib 1 (2: 3: 4: 3).
Rib 1 row.
Change to B.
Rib 1 row.
Bind off in rib.

finishing

Sew sleeves into armholes with row ends above markers sewn to sts bound off at underarm. Sew side and sleeve seams. Sew on buttons.

hooded jacket

hooded jacket   ●   ●   ●   ●   ●   ●   ●   ●   ●   ●   ●   ▷

sizes and measurements
To fit ages 3–6 (6–9: 9–12: 12–18: 18–24) months
knitted measurements
Chest 19¾ (21¼: 23¼: 25¼: 27½)in
Length to shoulder 10¾ (11½: 12½: 13¾: 15¼)in
Sleeve length with rolled edge 5½ (6¼: 7: 8¼: 9)in

materials
4 (5: 6: 6: 7) x 1¾oz/50g balls of Debbie Bliss Cashmerino Aran in apple green
Long circular and pair of size 8 knitting needles
One large button

gauge
18 sts and 24 rows to 4in square over St st using size 8 needles.

abbreviations
yo2 = yarn around right needle twice to make two new loops.
See page 27.

back
With size 8 needles, cast on 57 (61: 67: 73: 81) sts.
Beg with a k row, work in St st.
Work 6 rows.
Dec row K4, skp, k to last 6 sts, k2tog, k4.
Work 5 rows.
Rep the last 6 rows 3 (3: 4: 5: 6) times more and the dec row again. **47 (51: 55: 59: 65) sts.**
Work even until back measures 5½ (6: 7: 8: 9)in from cast-on edge, ending with a p row.
Shape armholes
Bind off 4 (4: 5: 5: 6) sts at beg of next 2 rows.
Leave the rem 39 (43: 45: 49: 53) sts on a spare needle.

left front
With size 8 needles, cast on 31 (33: 36: 39: 43) sts.
Next row K to end.
Next row K1, p to end.
These 2 rows set the St st with garter st edging.
Work 4 rows.
Dec row K4, skp, k to end.
Work 5 rows.
Rep the last 6 rows 3 (3: 4: 5: 6) times more and the dec row again. **26 (28: 30: 32: 35) sts.**
Work even until front measures 5½ (6: 7: 8: 9)in from cast-on edge, ending with a wrong side row.
Shape armhole
Bind off 4 (4: 5: 5: 6) sts at beg of next row.
Work 1 row.
Leave the rem 22 (24: 25: 27: 29) sts on a spare needle.

right front

With size 8 needles, cast on 31 (33: 36: 39: 43) sts.
Next row K to end.
Next row P to last st, k1.
These 2 rows set the St st with garter st edging.
Work 4 rows.
Dec row K to last 6 sts, k2tog, k4.
Work 5 rows.
Rep the last 6 rows 3 (3: 4: 5: 6) times more and the dec row again. **26 (28: 30: 32: 35) sts.**
Work even until front measures 5$\frac{1}{2}$ (6: 7: 8: 9)in from cast-on edge, ending with a right side row.
Shape armhole
Bind off 4 (4: 5: 5: 6) sts at beg of next row.
Leave the rem 22 (24: 25: 27: 29) sts on a spare needle. Do not break off yarn.

sleeves

With size 8 needles, cast on 30 (32: 34: 36: 38) sts.
Beg with a k row, work in St st.
Work 8 (8: 8: 10: 10) rows.
Inc row K3, M1, k to last 3 sts, M1, k3.
Work 3 rows in St st.
Rep the last 4 rows 5 (6: 7: 8: 9) times more and the inc row again. **44 (48: 52: 56: 60) sts.**
Work even until sleeve measures 5$\frac{1}{2}$ (6$\frac{1}{4}$: 7: 8$\frac{1}{4}$: 9)in from cast-on edge, ending with a p row.
Shape top of sleeve
Bind off 4 (4: 5: 5: 6) sts at beg of next 2 rows.
Leave rem 36 (40: 42: 46: 48) sts on a holder.

yoke

With right side facing and size 8 circular needle, work across right front, sleeve, back, sleeve, and left front as foll: k21 (23: 24: 26: 28) sts from right front, k last st tog with first st of sleeve, k34 (38: 40: 44: 46), k last st tog with first st of back, k37 (41: 43: 47: 51), k last st with first st of sleeve, k34 (38: 40: 44: 46), k last st tog with first st of left front, k21 (23: 24: 26: 28). **151 (167: 175: 191: 203) sts.**
Work backward and forward in rows.
Next row K1, p to last st, k1.
Next row K18 (20: 21: 23: 25), k2tog, k3, skp, k28 (32: 34: 38: 40), k2tog, k3, skp, k31 (35: 37: 41: 45), k2tog, k3, skp, k28 (32: 34: 38: 40), k2tog, k3, skp, k18 (20: 21: 23: 25). **143 (159: 167: 183: 195) sts.**
Next row K1, p to last st, k1.
Next row K17 (19: 20: 22: 24), k2tog, k3, skp, k26 (30: 32: 36: 38), k2tog, k3, skp, k29 (33: 35: 39: 43), k2tog, k3, skp, k26 (30: 32: 36: 38), k2tog, k3, skp, k17 (19: 20: 22: 24). **135 (151: 159: 175: 187) sts.**
Next row K1, p to last st, k1.
Next row K16 (18: 19: 21: 23), k2tog, k3, skp, k24 (28: 30: 34: 36), k2tog, k3, skp, k27 (31: 33: 37: 41), k2tog, k3, skp, k24 (28: 30: 34: 36), k2tog, k3, skp, k16 (18: 19: 21: 23). **127 (143: 151: 167: 179) sts.**
Next row K1, p to last st, k1.
Next row K15 (17: 18: 20: 22), k2tog, k3, skp, k22 (26: 28: 32: 34), k2tog, k3, skp, k25 (29: 31: 35: 39), k2tog, k3, skp, k22 (26: 28: 32: 34), k2tog, k3, skp, k15 (17: 18: 20: 22). **119 (135: 143: 159: 171) sts.**
Cont in this way dec 8 sts on every right side row until 71 (79: 87: 95: 99) sts rem, ending with a wrong side row.
Buttonhole row K2, k2tog, yo2, skp, work to end, dec as set.

Next row Work to end, working twice into yo2.
Work 4 (4: 6 :6: 6) more rows, dec on the next row and 1 (1: 2: 2: 2) foll right side rows as set.
47 (55: 55: 63: 67) sts.

Shape hood
Next row (right side) K9 (10: 10: 12: 12), bind off next 29 (35: 35: 39: 43) sts, k to end.
Next row K1, p8 (9: 9: 11: 11), cast on 56 (60: 60: 66: 72) sts, p8 (9: 9: 11: 11), k1. **74 (80: 80: 90: 96) sts.**
Next row K to end.
Next row K1, p to last st, k1.
Rep the last 2 rows 18 (19: 21: 22: 23) times more.

Shape top
Next row K34 (37: 37: 42: 45), k2tog, k2, skp, k34 (37: 37: 42: 45).
Next row K1, p32 (35: 35: 40: 43), p2tog tbl, p2, p2tog, p32 (35: 35: 40: 43), k1.
Next row K32 (35: 35: 40: 43), k2tog, k2, skp, k32 (35: 35: 40: 43).
Next row K1, p30 (33: 33: 38: 41), p2tog tbl, p2, p2tog, p30 (33: 33: 38: 41), k1.
Next row K30 (33: 33: 38: 41), k2tog, k2, skp, k30 (33: 33: 38: 41).
Next row K1, p28 (31: 31: 36: 39), p2tog tbl, p2, p2tog, p28 (31: 31: 36: 39), k1.
Next row K28 (31: 31: 36: 39), k2tog, k2, skp, k28 (31: 31: 36: 39).
Next row K1, p26 (29: 29: 34: 37), p2tog tbl, p2, p2tog, p26 (29: 29: 34: 37), k1.
Bind off.

finishing

Sew side and sleeve seams. Sew underarm seam. Fold bound-off edge of hood in half and sew seam. Easing in fullness, sew cast-on edge of hood to bound-off edge of back neck. Sew on button.

cable tank top

sizes and measurements

To fit ages 3–6 (6–9: 9–12: 12–18: 18–24) months

knitted measurements

Chest $17^3/_4$ (19: $20^1/_2$: 22: $23^1/_2$)in

Length to shoulder $8^3/_4$ ($9^1/_2$: $10^1/_4$: 12: $12^1/_2$)in

materials

2 (2: 2: 3: 3) x $1^3/_4$oz/50g balls of Debbie Bliss Baby Cashmerino in indigo

Pair each of sizes 2 and 3 knitting needles

Size 2 circular needle

Cable needle

2 small buttons

gauge

32 sts and 34 rows to 4in square over patt using size 3 needles.

abbreviations

C4B = slip next 2 sts onto cable needle and hold at back of work, k2, then k2 from cable needle.

See page 27.

back

** With size 3 needles, cast on 74 (80: 86: 92: 98) sts.

1st row (right side) [K2, p1] 1 (2: 3: 4: 5) times, [k4, p1, k2, p1] 8 times, k4, [p1, k2] 1 (2: 3: 4: 5) times.

2nd row [P2, k1] 1 (2: 3: 4: 5) times, [p4, k1, p2, k1] 8 times, p4, [k1, p2] 1 (2: 3: 4: 5) times.

3rd row [K2, p1] 1 (2: 3: 4: 5) times, [C4B, p1, k2, p1] 8 times, C4B, [p1, k2] 1 (2: 3: 4: 5) times.

4th row As 2nd row.

These 4 rows form the cable and rib patt and are repeated throughout.

Work in patt until back measures $4^3/_4$ (5: $5^1/_2$: $6^3/_4$: $7^1/_2$)in from cast-on edge, ending with a wrong side row.

Shape armholes

Bind off 4 (4: 5: 5: 6) sts at beg of next 2 rows. **66 (72: 76: 82: 86) sts.**

Dec 1 st at each end of the next and 5 (5: 7: 7: 7) foll alt rows. **54 (60: 60: 66: 70) sts.** **

Work even in patt as now set until back measures $6^3/_4$ ($7^1/_2$: $8^1/_4$: $9^1/_2$: $10^1/_4$)in from cast-on edge, ending with a wrong side row.

Divide for neck opening

Next row Patt 24 (27: 27: 30: 32), turn and cast on 5 sts.

Cont on these 29 (32: 32: 35: 37) sts only for first side of neck, leave rem sts on a spare needle.

Next row (wrong side) K1, p3, k1, patt to end.

Next row Patt to last 5 sts, p1, k3, p1.

Rep these 2 rows until back measures $8^1/_4$ (9: $9^3/_4$: $11^1/_2$: $12^1/_4$)in from cast-on edge, ending with a wrong side row.

Shape back neck

Next 2 rows Patt to last 10 sts, slip these sts onto a holder, turn and patt to end.

Next 2 rows Patt to last 5 sts, slip these sts onto same holder, turn and patt to end.

14 (17: 17: 20: 22) sts.

Bind off rem sts for shoulder, working 2 sts tog in center of each cable.

With right side facing, rejoin yarn to 30 (33: 33: 36: 38) sts on spare needle, patt to end.

Patt 7 rows.

Buttonhole row (right side) P1, k1, yo, k2tog, patt to end.

Cont in patt until back measures $8^1/_4$ (9: $9^3/_4$: $11^1/_2$: $12^1/_4$)in from cast-on edge, ending with a wrong side row.

Shape back neck

Next row (right side) Patt 11 and slip these sts onto a holder, patt to end.

Patt 1 row.

Next row Patt 5 and slip these sts onto the same holder, patt to end.

Patt 1 row. **14 (17: 17: 20: 22) sts.**

Bind off rem sts for shoulder, working 2 sts tog in center of each cable.

front

Work as given for Back from ** to **.

Work even in patt until front measures $6^1/_4$ (7: $7^3/_4$: 9: $9^3/_4$)in from cast-on edge, ending with a wrong side row.

Shape neck

Next row Patt 21 (24: 24: 27: 29) sts, turn and work on these sts only for first side of front neck.

Next row (wrong side) Bind off 2 sts, patt to end.
Patt 1 row.
Rep the last 2 rows once more.
Next row (wrong side) P1, p2tog, patt to end.
Next row Patt to last 2 sts, k2.
Rep the last 2 rows twice more. **14 (17: 17: 20: 22) sts.**
Work even until front measures same as Back to shoulder, ending with a wrong side row.
Bind off, working 2 sts tog in center of each cable.
With right side facing, slip center 12 sts onto a holder, rejoin yarn to rem sts, patt to end.
Patt 1 row.
Next row Bind off 2 sts, patt to end.
Patt 1 row.
Rep the last 2 rows once more.
Next row K1, skp, patt to end.
Next row Patt to last 2 sts, p2.
Rep the last 2 rows twice more. **14 (17: 17: 20: 22) sts.**
Work even until front measures same as Back to shoulder, ending with a right side row.

neckband

Bind off, working 2 sts tog in center of each cable.

Sew shoulder seams.

With right side facing and size 2 circular needle, work across 16 sts on left back neck holder as foll: [p1, patt 4, p1, k2] twice, then pick up 2 sts at back neck edge to shoulder, and k16 (19: 19: 22: 22) sts down left front neck, work [p1, k2, p1, k4, p1, k2, p1] across 12 sts from front neck holder, now pick up and k16 (19: 19: 22: 22) sts up right front neck, 2 sts from back neck edge then work across 15 sts on right back neck holder as foll: k2, p1, patt 4, p1, k2, p1, k3, p1. **79 (85: 85: 91: 91) sts.**

1st row (wrong side) K1, p3, k1, p2, k1, p4, [k1, p2] 8 (9: 9: 10: 10) times, k1, p4, k1, [p2, k1] 8 (9: 9: 10: 10) times, p4, k1, p2, k1, p4, k1.

Buttonhole row P1, k1, yo, k2tog, k1, p1, k2, p1, C4B, [p1, k2] 8 (9: 9: 10: 10) times, p1, C4B, p1, [k2, p1] 8 (9: 9: 10: 11) times, C4B, p1, k2, p1, k3, p1.

3rd row Rep 1st row.

4th row [P1, k4, p1, k2] twice, [p1, k2] 7 (8: 8: 9: 9) times, p1, k4, p1, [k2, p1] 8 (9: 9: 10: 10) times, k4, p1, k2, p1, k3, p1.

Bind off in patt, working [p2tog] twice across each cable while binding off.

armbands

With right side facing and size 2 needles, pick up and k62 (68: 74: 86: 92) sts evenly around armhole edge.

1st row (wrong side) [P2, k1] 3 (4: 5: 7: 8) times, [p4, k1, p2, k1] 5 times, p4, [k1, p2] 3 (4: 5: 7: 8) times.

2nd row [K2, p1] 3 (4: 5: 7: 8) times, [k4, p1, k2, p1] 5 times, k4, [p1, k2] 3 (4: 5: 7: 8) times.

3rd row Rep 1st row.

4th row [K2, p1] 3 (4: 5: 7: 8) times, [C4B, p1, k2, p1] 5 times, C4B, [p1, k2] 3 (4: 5: 7: 8) times.

Bind off in patt, working [p2tog] twice across each cable while binding off.

finishing

Sew side and armband seams. Stitch cast-on sts at back opening behind buttonhole band.

Sew on buttons.

sizes
To fit ages 0–3 (3-6: 6–9: 9–12: 12–24) months

materials
1 x 1³/₄oz/50g ball of Debbie Bliss Baby Cashmerino in each of main color (M) and contrasting color (C)
Set of four double-pointed knitting needles in each of sizes 5 and 3

gauge
25 sts and 34 rows to 4in square over St st using size 3 needles.

pixie hat

finishing

With a set of four size 5 double-pointed needles and M, cast on 88 (96: 104: 112: 120) sts.
Arrange sts on 3 of 4 needles and place a marker after last st to indicate end of rounds.
Taking care not to twist the edge, work in rounds of k1, p1 rib for ³/₄ (³/₄: 1¹/₄: 1¹/₄: 1¹/₄)in.
Change to set of four size 3 needles and C and cont to work ¹/₂in more in rounds of rib.
Working in rounds of St st (k every round) and stripe patt of 2 rounds C, 2 rounds M throughout, work even until work measures 4³/₄ (4³/₄: 5¹/₂: 5¹/₂: 6¹/₄)in from cast-on edge.
Shape top
Dec round [K20 (22: 24: 26: 28), k2tog] 4 times. **84 (92: 100: 108: 116) sts.**
Work 2 rounds.
Dec round [K19 (21: 23: 25: 27), k2tog] 4 times. **80 (88: 96: 104: 112) sts.**
Work 2 rounds.
Dec round [K18 (20: 22: 24: 26), k2tog] 4 times. **76 (84: 92: 100: 108) sts.**
Work 2 rounds.
Cont in this way to dec 4 sts as set on next and every 3rd round until 40 (44: 48: 52: 56) sts rem.
Work 1 round.
Cont to dec 4 sts as before on next round and every foll alt round until 8 sts rem.
Dec round [K2tog] 4 times. 4 sts.
Break off yarn, thread through rem sts, pull to gather, and secure.
Make a pompon in M and sew to top of hat.

sizes

To fit ages 3–6 (6–12: 12–18) months

materials

1 x 1³/₄oz/50g ball of Debbie Bliss Baby Cashmerino in each of main color (M) and contrasting color (C)
Set of four double-pointed size 3 knitting needles

gauge

25 sts and 34 rows to 4in square over St st using size 3 needles.

abbreviations

See page 27.

two tone socks

to make

With size 3 needles and C, cast on 32 (36: 40) sts.
Arrange these sts on 3 needles and cont in rounds.
Rib round * K1, p1; rep from * to end.
Work 3 (5: 7) rounds more in rib.
Change to M.
Now work in rounds of k, so forming St st.
K 2 (2: 4) rounds.
Dec round K5, k2tog, k to last 7 sts, skp, k5. **30 (34: 38) sts.**
K 3 (5: 7) rounds.
Dec round K4, k2tog, k to last 6 sts, skp, k4. **28 (32: 36) sts.**
Work 3 (5: 7) rounds.
Dec round K3, k2tog, k5 (6: 7), k2tog, [k5 (6: 7), skp] twice, k2 (3: 4). **24 (28: 32) sts.**
Break off M.
Divide sts onto 3 needles as foll: slip first 7 (8: 9) sts onto first needle,
next 5 (6: 7) sts onto second needle and next 5 (6: 7) sts onto 3rd needle, then
slip last 7 (8: 9) sts onto other end of first needle.

Shape heel

With right side facing, join C to 14 (16: 18) sts on first needle.

Cont in St st rows on these 14 (16: 18) sts only.

Beg with a k row, work 10 rows St st.

Next row K9 (11: 13), skp, turn.

Next row Sl 1, p4 (6: 8), p2tog, turn.

Next row Sl 1, k4 (6: 8), skp, turn.

Next row Sl 1, p4 (6: 8), p2tog, turn.

Rep the last 2 rows twice more. **6 (8: 10) sts.**

Break off yarn.

Reset sts on 3 needles as foll: slip first 3(4: 5) sts of heel sts onto a safety pin, place marker here to indicate beg of round. Join M to rem sts, with first needle k3(4: 5), then pick up and k8 sts along side of heel, with second needle k10(12: 14), with 3rd needle pick up and k8 sts along other side of heel, k3(4: 5) from safety pin. **32 (36: 40) sts.**

Cont in rounds.

K 1 round.

Dec round K9 (10: 11), k2tog, k10 (12: 14), k2tog tbl, k9 (10: 11). **30 (34: 38) sts.**

K 1 round.

Dec round K8 (9: 10), k2tog, k10 (12: 14), k2tog tbl, k8 (9: 10). **28 (32: 36) sts.**

K 1 round.

Dec round K7 (8: 9), k2tog, k10 (12: 14), k2tog tbl, k7 (8: 9). **26 (30: 34) sts.**

K 1 round.

Dec round K6 (7: 8), k2tog, k10 (12: 14), k2tog tbl, k6 (7: 8). **24 (28: 32) sts.**

Work even for 11 (13: 17) rounds.

Shape toe

Dec round [K2tog tbl, k4 (5: 6)] 4 times. **20 (24: 28) sts.**

K 1 round.

Dec round [K2tog tbl, k3 (4: 5)] 4 times. **16 (20: 24) sts.**

K 1 round.

Change to C.

Dec round [K2tog tbl, k2 (3: 4)] 4 times. **12 (16: 20) sts.**

K 1 round.

2nd and 3rd sizes only

Dec round [K2tog tbl, k- (2: 3)] 4 times. - (12: 16) sts.

3rd size only

K 1 round.

Dec round [K2tog tbl, k- (-: 2)] 4 times. – (-: 12) sts.

K 1 round.

All sizes

Dec round [K2tog tbl] 6 times.

Break off yarn, thread through rem 6 sts, pull to gather, and secure.

daisy cardigan

sizes and measurements

To fit ages 0–3 (3–6: 6–9: 9–12: 12–18: 18–24) months

knitted measurements

Chest 19^1/$_4$ (20^3/$_4$: 22^1/$_2$: 24: 25^1/$_2$: 27^1/$_4$)in

Length to shoulder 8^1/$_4$ (9^1/$_2$: 10^1/$_4$: 11: 12^1/$_2$: 14^1/$_4$)in

Sleeve length 5 (6: 6^3/$_4$: 7^1/$_2$: 8^3/$_4$: 9^1/$_2$)in

materials

5 (5: 6: 6: 7: 8) x 1^3/$_4$oz/50g balls of Debbie Bliss Cotton Double Knitting in pale green

Scraps of contrasting yarn for embroidery

Pair each sizes 3 and 6 knitting needles

5 (6: 6: 6: 7: 7) buttons

gauge

20 sts and 32 rows to 4in square over seed st using size 6 needles.

abbreviations

See page 27.

back

With size 3 needles, cast on 51 (55: 59: 63: 67: 71) sts.
K 5 rows.
Change to size 6 needles.
Seed st row * P1, k1; rep from * to last st, p1.
This row forms seed st and is repeated.
Work 3 more rows.
Eyelet row Seed st 1 (3: 5: 1: 3: 5), yo, p2tog, * seed st 4, yo, p2tog; rep from * to last
0 (2: 4: 0: 2: 4) sts, seed st 0 (2: 4: 0: 2: 4).
Cont in seed st until back measures $4^3/4$ ($5^1/2$: 6: $6^1/4$: $7^1/2$: $8^3/4$)in from cast-on edge, ending with a
wrong side row.
Shape armholes
Bind off 4 sts at beg of next 2 rows. **43 (47: 51: 55: 59: 63) sts.**
Work even until back measures $8^1/4$ ($9^1/2$: $10^1/4$: 11: $12^1/2$: $14^1/4$)in from cast-on edge, ending with a
wrong side row.
Shape shoulders
Bind off 10 (11: 13: 14: 16: 17) sts at beg of next 2 rows.
Bind off rem 23 (25: 25: 27: 27: 29) sts.

left front

With size 3 needles, cast on 28 (30: 32: 34: 36: 38) sts.
K 5 rows.
Change to size 6 needles.
1st row (right side) * P1, k1; rep from * to last 6 sts, p1, k5.
2nd row K5, p1, * k1, p1; rep from * to end.
These 2 rows form the seed st patt with garter st border.
Work 2 more rows.
Eyelet row Seed st 1 (3: 5: 1: 3: 5), yo, p2tog, * seed st 4, yo, p2tog; rep from * to last 7 sts, k1, p1, k5.
Cont in seed st with garter st border until front measures $4^3/4$ ($5^1/2$: 6: $6^1/4$: $7^1/2$: $8^3/4$)in from
cast-on edge, ending with a wrong side row.
Shape armhole
Bind off 4 sts at beg of next row. **24 (26: 28: 30: 32: 34) sts.**
Work even until front measures $6^3/4$ (8: $8^1/4$: 9: $10^1/4$: $11^3/4$)in from cast-on edge, ending with a
wrong side row.
Shape neck
Next row Patt to last 7 (7: 8: 8: 9: 9) sts, leave these sts on a holder for collar.
Dec 1 st at neck edge on every row until 10 (11: 13: 14: 16: 17) sts rem.
Work even until front measures same as Back to shoulder, ending at armhole edge.
Shape shoulder
Bind off.
Mark position for 5 (6: 6: 6: 7: 7) buttons, the first on the eyelet row, the last $1/2$in below neck edge,
with the rem 3 (4: 4: 4: 5: 5) spaced evenly between.

right front

With size 3 needles, cast on 28 (30: 32: 34: 36: 38) sts.

K 5 rows.

Change to size 6 needles.

1st row (right side) K5, p1, * k1, p1; rep from * to end.

2nd row * P1, k1; rep from * to last 6 sts, p1, k5.

These 2 rows form the seed st patt with garter st border.

Work 2 more rows.

Eyelet and buttonhole row (right side) K1, k2tog, yo, k2, p1, k1, yo, skp, * seed st 4, yo, skp; rep from * to last 1 (3: 5: 1: 3: 5) sts, seed st 1 (3: 5: 1: 3: 5) sts.

Cont in seed st with garter st border, working buttonholes to match left front markers, until front measures 4³/₄ (5¹/₂: 6: 6¹/₄: 7¹/₂: 8³/₄)in from cast-on edge, ending with a right side row.

Shape armhole

Bind off 4 sts at beg of next row. **24 (26: 28: 30: 32: 34) sts.**

Work even until front measures 6³/₄ (8: 8¹/₄: 9: 10¹/₄: 11³/₄)in from cast-on edge, ending with a wrong side row.

Shape neck

Next row Patt 7 (7: 8: 8: 9: 9) sts and leave these sts on a holder for collar, patt to end.

Dec 1 st at neck edge on every row until 10 (11: 13: 14: 16: 17) sts rem.

Work even until front measures same as Back to shoulder, ending at armhole edge.

Shape shoulder

Bind off.

sleeves

With size 3 needles, cast on 29 (31: 33: 35: 37: 39) sts.

K 5 rows.

Change to size 6 needles.

Seed st row (right side) P1, * k1, p1; rep from * to end.

This row forms the seed st and is repeated.

Work 3 more rows.

1st, 3rd 4th and 6th sizes only

Eyelet row Seed st 1 (–: 3: 1: –: 3), yo, p2tog, * seed st 4, yo, p2tog; rep from * to last 2 (–: 4: 2: –: 4) sts, seed st 2 (–: 4: 2: –: 4).

2nd and 5th sizes only

Eyelet row Seed st – (2: –: –: 2: –), yo, skp, * seed st 4, yo, skp; rep from * to last – (3: –: –: 3: –) sts, seed st – (3: –: –: 3: –).

All sizes

Cont in seed st and inc 1 st at each end of the next and every foll 6th (6th: 6th: 6th: 6th: 8th) row until there are 37 (41: 45: 49: 53: 55) sts, taking all inc sts into seed st.

Work even until sleeve measures 5 (6: 6³/₄: 7¹/₂: 8³/₄: 9¹/₂)in from cast-on edge, ending with a wrong side row.

Marking each end of last row with a colored thread.

Work 6 rows more.

Bind off.

collar

Sew shoulder seams.

With right side facing and size 3 needles, slip 7 (7: 8: 8: 9: 9) sts from right front neck holder onto a needle, pick up and k13 (13: 15: 15: 17: 17) sts up right front neck, k29 (31: 31: 33: 33: 35) sts from back neck edge, pick up and k13 (13: 15: 15: 17: 17) sts down left front neck, seed st 2 (2: 3: 3: 4: 4) sts, then k5 from left front holder. **69 (71: 77: 79: 85: 87) sts.**

Cont in seed st with 5 sts in garter st for borders.

Next 2 rows Patt to last 20 sts, turn.

Next 2 rows Patt to last 16 sts, turn.

Next 2 rows Patt to last 12 sts, turn.

Next 2 rows Patt to last 8 sts, turn.

Next row (wrong side) Patt to end.

Bind off 3 sts at beg of next 2 rows. **63 (65: 71: 73: 79: 81) sts.**

Cont in seed st with 2 sts in garter st for borders.

Work even for 1¹/₂ (1¹/₂: 1¹/₂: 2: 2: 2)in, ending with a wrong side row of collar.

Eyelet row (right side of collar) K2, seed st 2, yo, k2tog, patt to last 6 sts, k2tog, yo, seed st 2, k2.

Work 2 rows.

K 3 rows.

Bind off.

finishing

Using contrasting color, work buttonhole st around every buttonhole and eyelet. Sew sleeves into armholes with row-ends above colored threads sewn to sts bound off at underarm. Sew side and sleeve seams. Sew on buttons.

cable sweater

sizes and measurements
To fit ages 3–6 (6–9: 9–12: 12–18: 18–24) months
knitted measurements
Chest 19³/₄ (22¹/₂: 24: 26³/₄: 28³/₄)in
Length to shoulder 10¹/₄ (11: 11³/₄: 13: 14¹/₄)in
Sleeve length 6¹/₄ (7: 8: 8³/₄: 9¹/₂)in

materials
4 (4: 5: 5: 6) x 1³/₄oz/50g balls of Debbie Bliss Baby Cashmerino in pale blue (M) and 1 ball in ecru (C)
Pair each of sizes 2 and 3 knitting needles
Cable needle

gauge
25 sts and 34 rows to 4in square over St st using size 3 needles.

abbreviations
C4F = slip next 2 sts onto cable needle and hold at front of work, k2, then k2 from cable needle.
M1p = make one st by picking up and purling into back of loop between st just worked and next st.
See page 27.

back

With size 2 needles and C, cast on 74 (82: 90: 98: 106) sts.
1st row (right side) K2, * p2, k2; rep from * to end.
2nd row P2, * k2, p2; rep from * to end.
Change to M and work 4 rows more in rib.
Change to C and work 2 rows more in rib.
Change to M and work 1 row more in rib.
Inc row (wrong side) P2, k2 (0: 2: 0: 2), p2 (0: 2: 0: 2), * k2, M1p, p2, M1p, k2, p2; rep from * to last 4 (0: 4: 0: 4) sts, k2 (0: 2: 0: 2), p2 (0: 2: 0: 2). **90 (102: 110: 122: 130) sts.**
Change to size 3 needles.
Work in patt as foll:
1st row K2, p2 (0: 2: 0: 2), k2 (0: 2: 0: 2), * p2, k4, p2, k2; rep from * to last 4 (0: 4: 0: 4) sts, p2 (0: 2: 0: 2), k2 (0: 2: 0: 2).
2nd row P2, k2 (0: 2: 0: 2), p2 (0: 2: 0: 2), * k2, p4, k2, p2; rep from * to last 4 (0: 4: 0: 4) sts, k2 (0: 2: 0: 2), p2 (0: 2: 0: 2).
3rd row K2, p2 (0: 2: 0: 2), k2 (0: 2: 0: 2), * p2, C4F, p2, k2; rep from * to last 4 (0: 4: 0: 4) sts, p2 (0: 2: 0: 2), k2 (0: 2: 0: 2).
4th row Rep 2nd row.
5th row K2, p2 (0: 2: 0: 2), k2 (0: 2: 0: 2), * p2, k4, p2, k2; rep from * to last 4 (0: 4: 0: 4) sts, p2 (0: 2: 0: 2), k2 (0: 2: 0: 2).
6th row Rep 2nd row.
These 6 rows form the patt.
Cont in patt until back measures 6 (6$^1/_4$: 6$^3/_4$: 7$^1/_2$: 8$^1/_4$)in from cast-on edge, ending with a wrong side row.
Shape armholes
Bind off 3 sts at beg of next 2 rows. **84 (96: 104: 116: 124) sts.****
Cont in patt until back measures 10$^1/_4$ (11: 11$^3/_4$: 13: 14$^1/_4$)in from cast-on edge, ending with a wrong side row.
Shape shoulders
Bind off 13 (15: 16: 18: 19) sts at beg of next 4 rows.
Leave rem 32 (36: 40: 44: 48) sts on a holder.

front

Work as given for Back to **.
Shape front neck
Next row (right side) Patt 39 (45: 49: 55: 59) sts, k2tog, turn and work on these sts for first side of front neck.
Next row Patt to end.
Next row Patt to last 2 sts, k2tog.
Rep the last 2 rows until 26 (30: 32: 36: 38) sts rem.
Work even until front measures same as Back to shoulder, ending at armhole edge.
Shape shoulder
Bind off 13 (15: 16: 18: 19) sts at beg of next row.
Work 1 row.
Bind off rem 13 (15: 16: 18: 19) sts.
With right side facing, slip center 2 sts onto a safety pin, join yarn to rem sts, skp, patt to end.

Next row Patt to end
Next row Skp, patt to end.
Rep the last 2 rows until 26 (30: 32: 36: 38) sts rem.
Work even until front measures same as Back to shoulder, ending at armhole edge.
Shape shoulder
Bind off 13 (15: 16: 18: 19) sts at beg of next row.
Work 1 row.
Bind off rem 13 (15: 16: 18: 19) sts.

sleeves

With size 2 needles and C, cast on 34 (42: 42: 50: 50) sts.
1st row (right side) K2, * p2, k2; rep from * to end.
2nd row P2, * k2, p2; rep from * to end.
Change to M and work 4 rows more in rib.
Change to C and work 2 rows more in rib.
Change to M and work 1 row more in rib.
Inc row (wrong side) P2, * k2, M1p, p2, M1p, k2, p2; rep from * to end. 42 (52: 52: 62: 62) sts.
Change to size 3 needles.
Work in patt as foll:
1st row (right side) K2, * p2, k4, p2, k2; rep from * to end.
2nd row P2, * k2, p4, k2, p2; rep from * to end.
3rd row K2, * p2, C4F, p2, k2; rep from * to end.
4th row Rep 2nd row.
5th row K2, * p2, k4, p2, k2; rep from * to end.
6th row Rep 2nd row.

These 6 rows set the patt.
Inc and work into patt 1 st at each end of the next (3rd: next: 5th: next) row and every foll
3rd (4th: 3rd: 3rd: 3rd) row until there are 62 (72: 82: 92: 102) sts.
Work even until sleeve measures 6¼ (7: 8: 8¾: 9½)in from cast-on edge, ending with a wrong
side row.
Mark each end of last row with a colored thread.
Work 4 rows more.
Bind off.

neckband

Sew right shoulder seam.
With right side facing, size 2 needles, and M, pick up and k40 (43: 45: 47: 49) sts evenly down left
side of front neck, k2 from safety pin, pick up and k38 (41: 43: 45: 47) sts evenly up right side of
front neck, k0 (0: 0: 0: 1), p0 (0: 0: 1: 2), k0 (0: 1: 2: 2), p0 (1: 2: 2: 2), k1 (0: 0: 0: 0), [k2tog]
1 (2: 2: 2: 2) times, p2, k2, p2, [k2tog] twice, p2, k2, p2, [k2tog] twice, p2, k2, p2, [k2tog] 1 (2: 2: 2: 2)
times, k1 (0: 0: 0: 0), p0 (1: 2: 2: 2), k0 (0: 1: 2: 2), p0 (0: 0: 1: 2), k0 (0: 0: 0: 1) across back neck sts.
106 (114: 122: 130: 138) sts.
Change to C.
1st size only
1st row P2, * k2, p2; rep from * to end.
2nd and 4th sizes only
1st row K1, * p2, k2; rep from * to last st, p1.
3rd and 5th sizes only
1st row P1,* k2, p2; rep from * to last st, k1.
All sizes
This row sets the rib patt.
2nd row Rib 39 (42: 44: 46: 48), k2tog, skp, rib to end.
Change to M.
3rd row Rib to end.
4th row Rib 38 (41: 43: 45: 47), k2tog, skp, rib to end
Change to C.
5th row Rib to end.
6th row Rib 37 (40: 42: 44: 46), k2tog, skp, rib to end.
7th row Rib to end.
8th row Rib 36 (39: 41: 43: 45), k2tog, skp, rib to end.
Change to M.
9th row Rib to end.
Bind off in rib, while decreasing as before.

finishing

Sew left shoulder and neckband seam. Sew sleeves into armholes with row-ends above markers
sewn to sts bound off at underarm. Sew side and sleeve seams.

roll edge jacket 133

sizes and measurements

To fit ages 3–6 (6–9: 9–12: 12–18: 18–24) months

knitted measurements

Chest 19 (21^1/$_4$: 23^1/$_2$: 26: 28^1/$_4$)in

Length to shoulder 13 (13^3/$_4$: 14^1/$_2$: 15: 16^1/$_4$)in

Sleeve length 5^1/$_2$ (6^1/$_4$: 7: 8: 8^3/$_4$)in

materials

6 (7: 8: 9: 10) x 1^3/$_4$oz/50g balls of Debbie Bliss Cotton Double Knitting in chocolate (M) and 1 ball in duck egg (C)
Pair of size 6 knitting needles
3 buttons

gauge

20 sts and 39 rows to 4in square over garter st using size 6 needles.

abbreviations

See page 27.

back

With size 6 needles and C, cast on 66 (72: 78: 84: 90) sts.
Beg with a k row, work 3 rows in St st.
Change to M and p 1 row.
K 6 (6: 8: 8: 8) rows.
Next row (right side) K6, skp, k to last 8 sts, k2tog, k6.
K 1 row.
Rep the last 8 (8: 10: 10: 10) rows, 7 times more. **50 (56: 62: 68: 74) sts.**
K 8 (12: 0: 4: 8) rows.
Shape armholes
Bind off 3 (3: 4: 4: 5) sts at beg of next 2 rows. **44 (50: 54: 60: 64) sts.**
K 2 rows.
Next row (right side) K2, skp, k to last 4 sts, k2tog, k2.
K 3 rows.
Rep the last 4 rows 9 (10: 11: 12: 13) times more. **24 (28: 30: 34: 36) sts.**
Leave sts on a holder.

left front

With size 6 needles and C, cast on 35 (38: 41: 44: 47) sts.
Beg with a k row, work 3 rows in St st.
Change to M and p 1 row.
K 6 (6: 8: 8: 8) rows.
Next row (right side) K6, skp, k to end.
K 1 row.
Rep the last 8 (8: 10: 10: 10) rows, 7 times more. **27 (30: 33: 36: 39) sts.**
K 8 (12: 0: 4: 8) rows.
Shape armhole
Bind off 3 (3: 4: 4: 5) sts at beg of next row. **24 (27: 29: 32: 34) sts.**
K 3 rows.
Next row (right side) K2, skp, k to end.
K 3 rows.
Rep the last 4 rows 3 (3: 3: 3: 4) times more. **20 (23: 25: 28: 29) sts.**
Next row (right side) K2, skp, k to end.
K 0 (0: 2: 2: 0) rows.
Shape neck
Next row (wrong side) Bind off 4 sts, k to end.
1st, 2nd and 5th sizes only
Next row K to last 4 sts, k2tog, k2.
K 1 row.
All sizes
Next row K2, skp, k to last 4 sts, k2tog, k2.
K 1 row.
Next row K to last 4 sts, k2tog, k2.
K 1 row.
Rep the last 4 rows 1 (2: 3: 4: 4) times more. **8 sts.**
Next row K2, skp, k2tog, k2. **6 sts.**

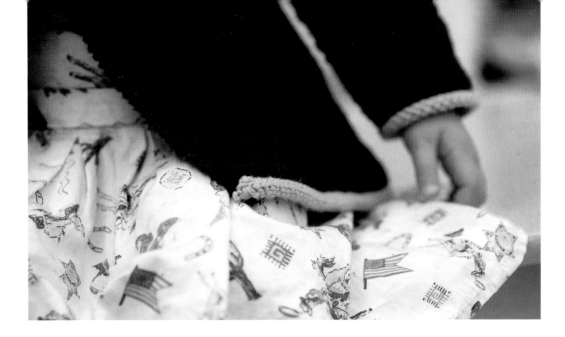

K 3 rows.
Next row K1, skp, k2tog, k1. **4 sts.**
K 3 rows.
Next row Skp, k2tog. **2 sts.**
K 3 rows.
Leave rem sts on a safety pin.

right front

With size 6 needles and C, cast on 35 (38: 41: 44: 47) sts.
Beg with a k row, work 3 rows in St st.
Change to M and p 1 row.
K 6 (6: 8: 8: 8) rows.
Next row (right side) K to last 8 sts, k2tog, k6.
K 1 row.
Rep the last 8 (8: 10: 10: 10) rows, 6 (6: 5: 5: 5) times more. **28 (31: 35: 38: 41) sts.**
K 2 (2: 4: 4: 6) rows.
1st buttonhole row (right side) K2, yo, k2tog, k to end.
K 3 (3: 3: 3: 1) rows.
Next row (right side) K to last 8 sts, k2tog, k6. **27 (30: 34: 37: 40) sts.**
3rd, 4th and 5th sizes only
K 9 rows.
Next row (right side) K to last 8 sts, k2tog, k6.
All sizes
K 10 (13: 2: 5: 9) rows.
2nd, 4th and 5th sizes only
2nd buttonhole row (right side): K2, yo, k2tog, k to end.
All sizes

Shape armhole

Next row (wrong side) Bind off 3 (3: 4: 4: 5) sts, k to end. 24 (27: 29: 32: 34) sts.

1st and 3rd sizes only

2nd buttonhole row (right side) K2, yo, k2tog, k to end.

All sizes

K 1 (2: 1: 2: 2) rows.

Next row (right side) K to last 4 sts, k2tog, k2.

K 3 rows.

Rep the last 4 rows 2 (2: 3: 3: 3) times more. 21 (24: 25: 28: 30) sts.

1st, 2nd and 5th sizes only

Next row (right side) K to last 4 sts, k2tog, k2.

K 1 row.

3rd buttonhole row (right side) K2, yo, k2tog, k to end.

K 1 row.

Next row K to last 4 sts, k2tog, k2.

K 1 row.

Shape neck

Next row (right side) Bind off 4 sts, with 1 st on needle, k1, skp, k to end.

K 1 row.

Next row K2, skp, k to last 4 sts, k2tog, k2.

K 1 row.

Next row K2, skp, k to end.

K 1 row.

3rd and 4th sizes only

3rd buttonhole row (right side) K2, yo, k2tog, k to last 4 sts, k2tog, k2.

K 3 rows.

Shape neck

Next row (right side) Bind off 4 sts, with 1 st on needle, k1, skp, k to last 4 sts, k2tog, k2.

K 1 row.

Next row (right side) K2, skp, k to end.

K 1 row.

Next row K2, skp, k to last 4 sts, k2tog, k2.

K 1 row. .

Next row (right side) K2, skp, k to end.

K 1 row.

All sizes

Rep the last 4 rows 1 (2: 2: 3: 4) times more. **8 sts.**

Next row K2, skp, k2tog, k2. **6 sts.**

K 3 rows.

Next row K1, skp, k2tog, k1. **4 sts.**

K 3 rows.

Next row Skp, k2tog. **2 sts.**

K 3 rows.

Leave rem sts on a safety pin.

sleeves

With size 6 needles and C, cast on 28 (30: 32: 32: 34) sts.

Beg with a k row, work 3 rows in St st.

Change to M and p 1 row.

Now work in garter st and inc 1 st at each end of 7th (11th: 11th: 11th: 11th) and every foll 8th row until there are 40 (42: 46: 48: 52) sts.

Work even until sleeve measures 5 (5$\frac{3}{4}$: 6$\frac{1}{2}$: 7$\frac{1}{2}$: 8$\frac{1}{4}$)in from start of garter st, ending with a wrong side row.

Shape raglans

Bind off 3 (3: 4: 4: 5) sts at beg of next 2 rows. **34 (36: 38: 40: 42) sts.**

K 2 rows.

Next row K2, skp, k to last 4 sts, k2tog, k2.

K 3 rows.

Rep the last 4 rows 3 (4: 5: 6: 7) times more. **26 sts.**

Next row K2, skp, k7, skp, k2tog, k7, k2tog, k2.

K 3 rows.

Next row K2, skp, k to last 4 sts, k2tog, k2. **20 sts.**

K 3 rows.

Next row K2, skp, k4, skp, k2tog, k4, k2tog, k2.

K 3 rows.

Next row K2, skp, k to last 4 sts, k2tog, k2. **14 sts.**

K 3 rows.

Next row K2, skp, k1, skp, k2tog, k1, k2tog, k2.

K 3 rows.

Next row K2, skp, k to last 4 sts, k2tog, k2. **8 sts.**

K 3 rows.

Leave rem 8 sts on a holder.

collar

Sew raglan seams.

With right side facing, size 6 needles, and M, beg 2 sts in from front edge, pick up and k13 (15: 15: 17: 19) sts up right front neck, k2tog from safety pin, work [k2tog, k4, k2tog] across 8 sts of right sleeve, work [k2tog, k5 (6: 7: 8: 8), k2tog, k6 (8: 8: 10: 12), k2tog, k5 (6: 7: 8: 8), k2tog] across 24 (28: 30: 34: 36) sts on back neck holder, work [k2tog, k4, k2tog] across sts of left sleeve, k2tog from safety pin, then pick up and k14 (16: 16: 18: 20) sts down left front neck, ending 2 sts in from front edge. **61 (69: 71: 79: 85) sts.**

1st row (wrong side) K all sts.

Change to C.

Beg with a k row, work 7 rows in St st.

Bind off.

finishing

Sew side and sleeve seams, reversing seam on contrast edges, allowing these to roll.

Sew on buttons.

yarn distributors

For suppliers of Debbie Bliss
yarns please contact:

USA
Knitting Fever Inc.
315 Bayview Avenue
Amityville, NY 11701
t: +1 516 546 3600
f: +1 516 546 6871
e: admin@knittingfever.com
w: www.knittingfever.com

CANADA
Diamond Yarns Ltd
155 Martin Ross Avenue Unit 3
Toronto
Ontario M3J 2L9
Canada
t: +1 416 736 6111
f: +1 416 736 6112
w. www.diamondyarn.com

MEXICO
Estambres Crochet SA de CV
Aaron Saenz 1891-7
Col. Santa Maria
Monterrey
N.L. 64650
Mexico
t: +52 (81) 8335 3870
e: abremer@redmundial.com.mx

BELGIUM/HOLLAND
Pavan
Meerlaanstraat 73
9860 Balegem (Oostrezele)
Belgium
t: +32 (0) 9 221 85 94
f: +32 (0) 9 221 56 62
e: pavan@pandora.be

ICELAND
Storkurinn
Langavegi 59
101 Reykjavik
Iceland
t: +354 551 8258
f: +354 562 8252

**GERMANY/AUSTRIA/
SWITZERLAND**
Designer Yarns
Handelsagentur Klaus Koch
Sachstraße 30
D-50259 Pulheim-Brauweiler
Germany
t: +49 (0) 2234 205453
f: +49 (0) 2234 205456
e: kk@designeryarns.de
w: www.designeryarns.de

FRANCE
Elle Tricote
8 Rue du Cocq
La Petite France
67000 Strasbourg
France
t: +33 (0) 388 230313
f: +33 (0) 8823 0169
w: www.elletricote.com

SPAIN
Oyambre
Pau Claris 145
08009 Barcelona
Spain
t: +34 934 87 2672
f: +34 67870 8614
e: marian@oyambreonline.com

SWEDEN/DENMARK/NORWAY
Hamilton Design
Storgatan 14
SE-64730 Mariefred
Sweden
t: +46 (0) 159 12006
f: +46 (0) 159 21805
w: www.hamiltondesign.biz

AUSTRALIA
Prestige Yarns Pty Ltd
PO Box 39
Bulli
NSW 2516
Australia
t: +61 (0) 2 4285 6669
e: info@prestigeyarns.com
w: www.prestigeyarns.com

FINLAND
Vilmiinan Villapouti
Nåsilinnankatu 23
33210 Tampere
Finland
t/f: +358 (0) 3 2129676
e: info@villapouti.net

JAPAN
Hobbyra Hobbyre
5-23-37 Higashi-Ohi
Shinagawa-ku
Tokyo 140-0011
Japan
t: +81 3 3472 1104
f: +81 3 3472 1196
w: www.hobbyra-hobbyre.com

UK
Designer Yarns Ltd
Units 8–10 Newbridge
Industrial Estate
Pitt Street
Keighley
West Yorkshire BD21 4PQ
UK
t: +44 (0) 1535 664222
f: +44 (0) 1535 664333
e: david@designeryarns.uk.com
w: www.designeryarns.uk.com

For more information about
my yarns, please visit
www.debbieblissonline.com

glossary of patterns

striped sweater pages 44–47

baby aged (months)	3–6	6–9	9–12
finished chest (in)	19¾	20¾	23¼
back length (in)	9½	10¼	11
sleeve length (in)	6¼	7	7¾

baby shrug pages 48–53

baby aged (months)	3–6	6–9	9–12	12–18	18–24
finished chest (in)	20	20¾	23½	25	27¼
back length (in)	9½	10¾	11½	12¼	13
sleeve length (in)	5	6	6¾	8	8¾

baby blanket pages 54–57

length (in)	23½
width (in)	21¼

crossover jacket pages 58–61

baby aged (months)	3–6	6–9	9–12	12–18	18–24
finished chest (in)	19¾	21¼	24	25¼	27½
back length (in)	9½	10¼	11½	12½	14¼
sleeve length (in)	5½	6¼	7	8	8¾

matinee coat pages 62–65

baby aged (months)	3–6	6–9	9–12
finished chest (in)	19¾	20¾	22
back length (in)	10¼	11	11¾
sleeve length (in)	6	6¼	6¾

teddy bear pages 66–69

height (in)	12

141

cuff bootees pages 70–73

baby aged (months)	0–3	3–6	6–9

cable yoke jacket pages 74–79

baby aged (months)	9–12	12–18	18–24
finished chest (in)	25½	27¼	29½
back length (in)	11¾	13½	15
sleeve length (in)	6¼	7	9

smock coat pages 80–85

baby aged (months)	3–6	6–12	12–18	24–36
finished chest (in)	23½	25½	26¾	28
back length (in)	14¼	15¼	17	19¾
sleeve length (in)	6¼	7	8	9

pompon beret pages 86–87

baby aged (months)	3–6	9–12	18–24

lace edge cardigan pages 88–91

baby aged (months)	3–6	6–9	9–12	12–18	18–24
finished chest (in)	19¾	21¼	23¼	24½	26¾
back length (in)	8¾	9½	10¼	11½	12½
sleeve length (in)	4¾	5½	6¼	7	7¾

cable blanket pages 92–95

length (in)	31½
width (in)	19¾

fair isle cardigan pages 96–101

baby aged (months)	3–6	6–9	9–12	12–18	18–24
finished chest (in)	18½	20½	22	24	26
back length (in)	8¾	9½	10¼	11	12½
sleeve length (in)	5	6	6¾	7½	8¾

hooded jacket pages 102–107

baby aged (months)	3–6	6–9	9–12	12–18	18–24
finished chest (in)	19¾	21¼	23¼	25¼	27½
back length (in)	10¾	11½	12½	13¾	15¼
sleeve length (in)	5½	6¼	7	8¼	9

cable tank top pages 108–113

baby aged (months)	3–6	6–9	9–12	12–18	18–24
finished chest (in)	17¾	19	20½	22	23½
back length (in)	8¾	9½	10¼	12	12½

pixie hat pages 114–115

baby aged (months)	0–3	3–6	6–9	9–12	12–24

two tone socks pages 116–119

baby aged (months)	3–6	6–12	12–18

daisy cardigan pages 120–125

baby aged (months)	0–3	3–6	6–9	9–12	12–18	18–24
finished chest (in)	19¼	20¾	22½	24	25½	27¼
back length (in)	8¼	9½	10¼	11	12½	14¼
sleeve length (in)	5	6	6¾	7½	8¾	9½

cable sweater pages 126–131

baby aged (months)	3–6	6–9	9–12	12–18	18–24
finished chest (in)	19¾	22½	24	26¾	28¾
back length (in)	10¼	11	11¾	13	14¼
sleeve length (in)	6¼	7	8	8¾	9½

roll edge jacket pages 132–138

baby aged (months)	3–6	6–9	9–12	12–18	18–24
finished chest (in)	19	21¼	23½	26	28¼
back length (in)	13	13¾	14½	15	16¼
sleeve length (in)	5½	6¼	7	8	8¾

Debbie Bliss is one of the foremost designers of hand knits. Her bestselling books have earned her a dedicated army of fans worldwide who adore her stylish, easy-to-make designs that have an enduring appeal. Debbie has published numerous books on knitting for both the home and all the family, including **Special Knits**, **Junior Knits** and **Debbie Bliss Home**, but it is designing knitwear for babies that really captures her imagination. Debbie continues to develop her own range of natural yarns for hand knits and to design highly wearable garments with universal appeal.

For a complete list of Debbie Bliss titles and other knitting books, contact:
Trafalgar Square Publishing
388 Howe Hill Road
North Pomfret, Vermont 05053
800.423.4525
www.trafalgarsquarebooks.com

acknowledgments

This book would not have been possible without the contribution of the following:

Jane O'Shea, Lisa Pendreigh, and **Mary Evans** at Quadrille Publishing whose combination of professional standards and incredible support have made this book such a joy to work on.

Julie Mansfield, the stylist, whose creative contribution to this book has been inspirational.

Tim Evan-Cook, whose wonderful photography and complete unflappability in the midst of the baby shoots created an oasis of calm, and his assistants Willem and Damien.

Sally Kvalheim, the baby groomer.

The wonderful babies, of course: **Abigail, Aidan, Elina, Florence, Genevieve, Ida, Jas, Jessica, Joshua Bentley, Joshua Roberts, Litzi, Louis, Louise, Mia,** and **Tyler.**

Rosy Tucker, for her design contribution, pattern checking, and all around essential input into all my projects.

Penny Hill, for her sterling work in pattern compiling and organizing the knitters, all under deadline pressure.

Marilyn Wilson, for the second pattern check.

The fantastic knitters, without whom, of course, none of this would happen: **Cynthia Brent, Pat Church, Jacqui Dunt, Shirley Kennet, Maisie Lawrence,** and **Frances Wallace.**

My fantastic agent, **Heather Jeeves.**

The **distributors, agents,** and **retailers** who support all my books and yarns, and of course, those knitters whose incredible support for my work over the years has made all this possible.